LEARN TO MAKE
HOME FURNISHINGS

Jane Newdick

COLLINS

The author thanks the following people and companies for their help with this book:
Julia James
Angela Aziz
Jeremy Way
Osborne & Little Ltd, Kings Road, London SW1 for fabrics (curtains, page 17, square and round tablecloths, page 5)
G. P. & J. Baker Ltd, PO Box 30, West End Road, High Wycombe, Bucks for fabrics (cushion covers, pages 8–9, roller blind, page 44)
Parkertex Fabrics Ltd, PO Box 30, West End Road, High Wycombe, Bucks for fabric (chair slip cover, page 20)
Laura Ashley PLC for fabric (headboard, page 32)
Cent Idées Magazine for photograph on page 54

First published in 1987
by William Collins Sons & Co Ltd
London · Glasgow · Sydney · Auckland · Johannesburg

Reprinted 1989

© Jane Newdick 1987

Designed by Mike Leaman
Photography by Di Lewis
Illustrated by Terry Evans and Margaret Leaman
Series Editor Eve Harlow

Newdick, Jane
Learn to make home furnishings. – (Learn a craft)
1. Drapery   2. Slip covers   3. Bedding
I. Title   II. Series
646.2'1   TT387

ISBN 0–00–412130–9

Typeset by Nene Phototypesetters Ltd
Printed by New Interlitho, Italy

Contents

Introduction

If you sew, the chances are that you have already tried your hand at making something for your home. It may have been a simple cushion or pillow cover or perhaps a more ambitious project such as a pair of curtains or drapes. This kind of homemaking sewing is very rewarding and an excellent opportunity to create home furnishings which reflect your individual sense of style.

The choice of fabrics available has never been better, in terms of design and suitability. Nowadays you can sew for every room in the house with fabrics and materials which look superb, wash or dryclean and are perfect for the job.

This book is planned for people with just a basic knowledge of sewing. Only a few simple seams are needed for the majority of projects and where special techniques are required, these are clearly explained and illustrated. Sewing for your home is not difficult to do, even when large amounts of fabric are involved, such as for curtains or for slip covers. You will find that the basic construction of most furnishings is simple and straightforward and, in many instances, easier to do than dressmaking.

The methods I have used throughout this book are tried and tested, and I have used them often in making furnishings for my own home. They are sometimes a little unorthodox but they will always produce excellent results.

Once you have successfully worked the basic technique, there is scope for you to try out ideas of your own. In this way, you can produce, room by room, beautifully made furnishings and accessories, in colours and designs which you have chosen to make your home very special and a reflection of your personality.

Dining Rooms

Ready-made tablecloths and place mats tend to come in standard sizes. Your table may not be a standard size and making your own table linen is a practical solution. This chapter shows how square and round tablecloths are made, with ideas for place mats and napkins.

Tablecloths

Square or rectangular tablecloths for small tables are simple to make. The edges are neatly hemmed, either by hand or with machine-stitching and little else needs to be done. However, as most fabrics, apart from sheeting and embroidery linen, are only 120cm (48in)-wide, tablecloths for tables larger than 90cm (36in) across have to be made by joining pieces of fabric. If this can be done by 'patchworking' two or more fabrics together (see pages 62–63) or by using an embroidery stitch for joining seams, the tablecloth becomes an attractive, as well as useful, dining room furnishing.

Square cloths can also be used on round tables, thrown over a full-length round cloth, as shown in the picture.

To produce a similar effect, make the square cloth big enough to cover the table top completely, with a good drop over the sides. As a guide, allow a 10cm (4in) drop from the table edge at the shortest point.

Finishing square cloths

A plain, neat edging is made by first pressing a narrow hem to the wrong side. Turn a second, deeper hem. Press, baste and then either machine-stitch or hem by hand. Corners should be neatly mitred (see page 7, Fig 3 for technique).

Round tablecloth

Once you have learned how to measure up and estimate for a round cloth, the technique can be adapted to make cloths of any size.

Measuring the table

First decide the depth of the cloth's overhang. For a small, decorative table, the cloth can go down to the floor. For a dining table, the overhang should be between 23–30cm (9–12in), so that diners' knees are clear of the edges.

Measure the diameter of the table top and add twice the overhang plus 5cm (2in) for the hem. You will need a square of fabric with sides of this measurement.

If the fabric you are using is narrower, widths or part widths must be joined together to obtain a square of the required size (see Fig 1).

Preparation

Measure and estimate fabric quantity as described, allowing an extra 15mm (5/8in) seam allowance on the edges to be joined.

Join pieces of fabric with straight seams. Press seams open and, if the fabric is likely to fray easily, neaten the seam edges.

Fold the prepared square of fabric in half and then in half again. Lay it on a flat surface. Pin the layers together on the edges and then pin a piece of thin string to the folded corner. Tie a chalk pencil to the end of the string and draw an arc, from corner to corner, as shown in Fig 2. Cut out on the chalked line, through all layers of fabric. Remove the pins and unfold the circle of fabric.

Making the tablecloth

The hem can be finished in different ways. Choose from one of the following:
1. Turn a narrow hem, then a 2cm (3/4in) hem to the wrong side. Hem by hand, pleating the fabric to take up the fullness (Fig 3).
2. Work zigzag machine-stitching along the raw edge. Turn the hem and baste. Work two rows of straight machine-stitching, 6mm (1/4in) apart.
3. Turn a 2.5cm (1in) hem, press and apply bias binding to cover the raw edges.

On decorative cloths, lace, broderie anglaise, braid or bobble fringing can be applied for a hem finish.

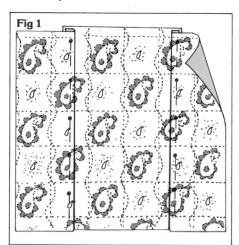

Fig 1 *When joining part-widths of fabric press under the selvedges on the two part-widths and pin over the middle width, matching the patterns on both edges. Baste then machine-stitch*

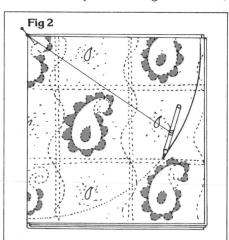

Fig 2 *Making a fabric circle: fold the fabric square twice. Pin thin twine to the folded corner. Tie on a pencil. Draw an arc*

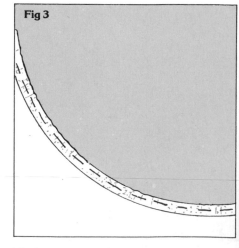

Fig 3 *Turn and baste a narrow doubled hem on the curved edge, easing in the fullness and keeping the edge smooth*

Place mats and napkins

White table linen gives an elegant touch to special occasions. In the picture, the linen has been embroidered in blue, the colour scheme taken from the china. Using a crisp piqué fabric with a squared pattern in the weave, it is a simple matter to follow the lines to work a machine-stitched decoration. Cream embroidery on white fabric would be a sophisticated variation.

Materials required

For six place mats 35 × 45cm (14 × 18in) and six napkins 45cm (18in) square

2.40m *(2⅝yd)* of 120cm *(48in)*-wide white cotton piqué fabric
Sewing thread, white, light blue and dark blue

Preparation

Press the creases from the fabric. Referring to Fig 1, measure and cut six rectangular place mats and six square napkins. Cut the mats 38 × 48cm *(15 × 19in)*. Cut the napkins 48cm *(19in)* square.

Working the design

Set the sewing machine to a wide, close satin stitch. Following the picture, work two rows of dark blue satin stitching round each of the place mats, setting the outer row 5cm *(2in)* from the edge.

The napkins have a motif in one corner, consisting of two squares, one in light blue and the other in dark blue thread. Fig 2 shows the direction of the satin stitching. Use the squared weave of the fabric as a guide to working the embroidery. If desired, a square motif could also be worked in one corner of the place mats.

Finishing

Fold and press a double 6mm *(¼in)* hem on all four sides of the place mats and napkins. Baste and machine-stitch, using white thread, stitching close to the edge. Mitre the corners, following Figs 3a, 3b and 3c.

Alternatively, a drawn thread edge could be worked for a pretty finish.

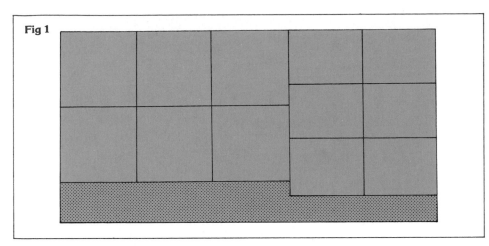

Fig 1

Fig 1 *Fabric layout for cutting 6 placemats and 6 napkins from 2.40m (2⅝yd) of 120cm (48in)-wide fabric*

Fig 2 *Work machine satin stitch along the squared weave lines of the fabric. Work the dark blue square first, then the light blue square*

Fig 3 *Mitring square corners on linen: fold and press a narrow hem to the wrong side (A). Fold the corner on the inner, broken diagonal line and trim off the corner on the outer broken line. Press the turning (B). Fold the hems in so that the folded edges meet. Hem. Machine-stitch the hem (C)*

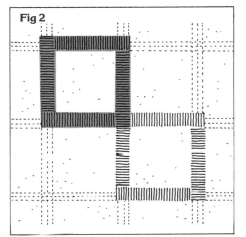

Fig 2

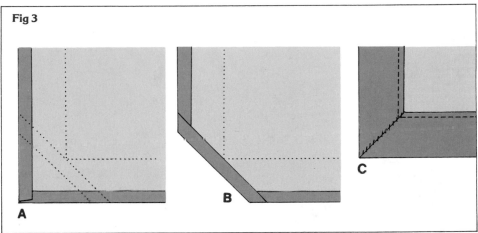

Fig 3

A

B

C

Decorative napkins and place mats

Napkins and place mats made from plain fabrics can be decorated in different ways.

1   Stitch strips of washable, colourfast ribbons down one edge or across one corner.

2   Form ribbons into flower shapes and catch the petals and flower centres to the fabric.

3   Cut motifs from patterned fabrics and apply them to the napkin corners with close zigzag machine-stitching.

4   Print seasonal motifs, such as Christmas bells and holly leaves using cut potatoes and fabric paint.

5   Allow the children to draw motifs and faces on napkins and place mats then embroider the outlines with simple stitches such as Stem stitch and Chain stitch.

6   For special occasions, a striking table setting can be made by catch-stitching guipure lace motifs to the corners of dark-toned place mats. Add a smaller motif to the corners of napkins to match.

Living Rooms

The opportunities for sewing for the living room are considerable – almost everything is made of, or includes, fabric. Comfortable cushions and pillows, pretty lampshades, professional-looking curtains and slip covers and simple upholstery are in this chapter.

Cushions and Pillows

Every home needs cushions for comfort but they are also excellent for adding colour and style to a room. Cushions can be of all kinds of shapes and sizes, from large, soft, floor cushions to small, lace-trimmed day bed cushions. The basic method of making a cushion cover is the same for most types of cushion.

Easy cushion

The simplest and easiest cushion cover for a beginner to make is a square shape.

Materials required
Square cushion pad
2 squares of fabric the size of the
   cushion pad
Matching sewing thread

Making the cushion
Pin the two pieces of fabric together round the edges, wrong sides facing, placing the pins 12mm (*1/2in*) from the edges. Baste round the cushion, removing the pins. Machine-stitch the seam starting 5cm (*2in*) from a corner. Stitch up to the corner, then along three sides and round the fourth corner for about 5cm (*2in*), as shown in Fig 1, page 10. Remove the basting. Trim the fabric at the corners (Fig 1). Press the seams, then turn the cushion cover to the right side. Press again. Insert the cushion pad. Turn in the seam allowance on the opening and pin, then baste to close the seam. Sew the seam with slipstitches or with oversewing.

Square piped cushion

Once you have made a simple, square cushion cover, you can go on to making professional-looking piped-edge cushions, such as those in the picture. Piping is not essential but it does give a hard-wearing finish, as well as giving scope for decoration with contrasting colours.

Materials required
Finished size 30cm (12in) square
30cm (*12in*)-square cushion pad
40cm (*16in*) of 120cm (*48in*)-wide
   fabric
1.40m (*1 1/2yd*) of piping cord
Matching sewing thread

Preparation
If the piping cord is made of cotton, it must be pre-shrunk. Tie the cord into a hank and simmer in hot water for 3 minutes. Roll in a towel to remove the excess water. Hang to dry.
   Cut two pieces of fabric 33cm (*13in*) square. From the remaining fabric cut bias strips for covering the piping cord.

Bias strips Spread the fabric and, using a ruler, chalk a line on the true diagonal of the fabric. Measure and mark parallel lines 4cm (*1 1/2in*) apart. Cut strips along the chalk lines. (Fig 2 page 10).

Joining bias strips Place two strips at right angles, right sides together. Machine-stitch (Fig 3). Open out and press. Trim the protruding corners of the seam allowance.

Making the cushion
Prepare the piping first. Lay the cord down the centre of the bias strip, on the wrong side. Fold the fabric over the cord and work basting stitches through both thicknesses of fabric, close up against the cord (Fig 4).
   Pin the piped cord to the right side of one of the fabric squares, matching the

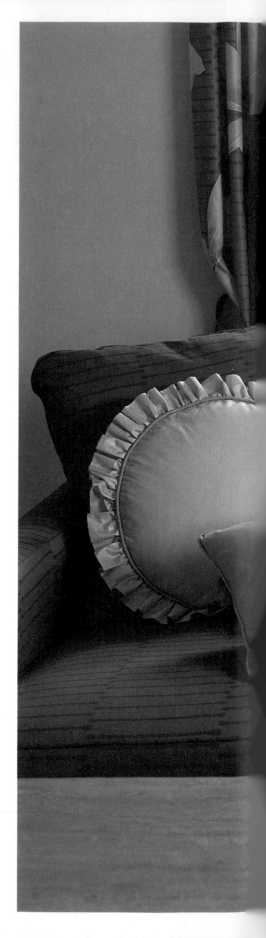

Fig 1

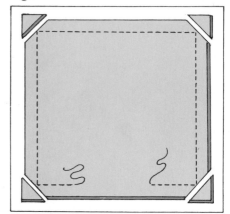

Fig 1 *Make simple cushions by machine-stitching 2 square pieces of fabric together. Begin 5cm (2in) from a corner, stitch to corner, pivot the needle, continue stitching 3 sides and then part of the fourth*

Fig 2

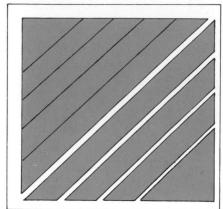

Fig 2 *Cutting bias strips: fold the fabric on the diagonal and chalk-mark the fold. Measure and mark diagonal lines. Cut strips along the lines*

Fig 3

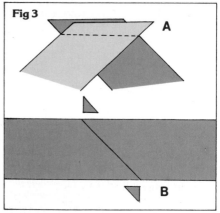

Fig 3 *Joining bias strips: pin 2 strips at right angles. Baste and machine-stitch (A). Press the seam open, trim off the protruding corners (B)*

Fig 4

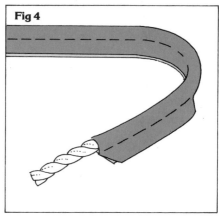

Fig 4 *Fold the bias strip round the cord and baste close to the cord through both thicknesses of fabric*

Fig 5

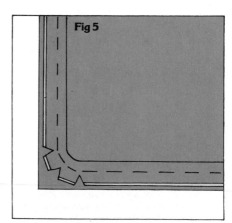

Fig 5 *Baste the piped cord to the right side of the cushion piece matching raw edges. Clip into the piping seam allowance at the corners for ease*

Fig 6

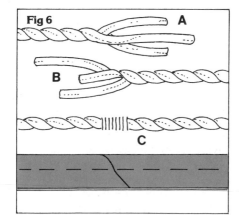

Fig 6 *Joining cord ends: unravel one cord end. Cut 2 threads to half the length (A). Cut 1 thread short on other end of cord (B). Twist together, oversew. Join piping seam by hand (C)*

raw edges of the fabric and the piping. You will need to clip into the raw edge of the piping fabric at the corners (see Fig 5). This helps the piping to form a neat, square corner. Baste the piping to the fabric. Machine-stitch, still working from the right side, using the machine's zipper foot. This enables you to stitch close to the piping.

Joining piping ends When you are nearing the point where the piping ends meet, remove the work from the machine.

Unravel the cord ends. From one end, cut two of the three threads to half their length. From the other cord end, cut one thread to half its length (Fig 6a). Twist the threads together and oversew (Fig 6b). Sew the piping fabric edges together by hand for a neat finish (Fig 6c). Complete the application of the piping with machine-stitching.

Finishing
Unpick the basting threads from the piping. Place the second square of fabric, right side down, on top, matching the edges. Pin and baste all round. Turn the work over and machine-stitch from this side, working over the same line of stitches as before, but stitching on three sides only. Leave the fourth side open. Remove the basting stitches and trim the fabric away at the corners to reduce bulk. Turn the cushion cover to the right side. Press. Insert the cushion pad. Close the open seam with slipstitches. If you prefer, the open seam can be finished with a zip fastener. See page 12, Fig 5.

Cushion pads
Cushion pads can be bought in different shapes – square, rectangular, round and heart-shaped – filled with kapok, feathers, feathers and down, foam chips or polyester padding. It is possible to make your own cushion pad and this is sometimes desirable if a specific size or shape is required.

To make a cushion pad, follow the technique described for making the Easy cushion. When the seams have been stitched, turn the pad to the right side through the open seam and fill it with the chosen filling. Finish the pad by closing the open seam with oversewing.

Frills and finishes

Simple, square cushions in plain colours make elegant room accessories, the fabric colours chosen to tone in with other furnishings. Sometimes, however, more decorative cushions are required, providing scope for the addition of frills, edgings, appliqué and embroidery.

Shell cushion

One of the square cushions in the picture on pages 8–9 has an appliquéd shell motif. The pattern for this is given in Fig 1.

Preparation

From the graph pattern (Fig 1) draw the shell on squared paper (scale 1sq = 2.5cm (1in). Trace the shape to the wrong side of the appliqué fabric using dressmaker's carbon paper.

Before cutting out the shape, work a narrow, close zigzag machine-stitch over all the lines.

Cut out the shape, close to the stitched outline.

Applying the motif

Appliqué, and all surface decoration, should be completed on the fabric before the cushion is made up.

Baste the prepared motif to the fabric. Work close zigzag machine-stitch over the edges. If a padded effect is required, insert scraps of washable polyester wadding under the motif before completing the satin stitching.

Frilled cushion

Frills can be applied to cushions of any shape. In the picture on pages 8–9, a round cushion is frilled.

Preparation

Cut out the front and back pieces of the cushion. From the remaining fabric cut strips to twice the desired depth of frill. Join strips to make a length twice the circumference of the cushion. Fold the strip, wrong sides facing, and work two rows of running stitches, close together, along the edges, and through both thicknesses of fabric (Fig 2).

Making the cushion

If the cushion is being piped, prepare

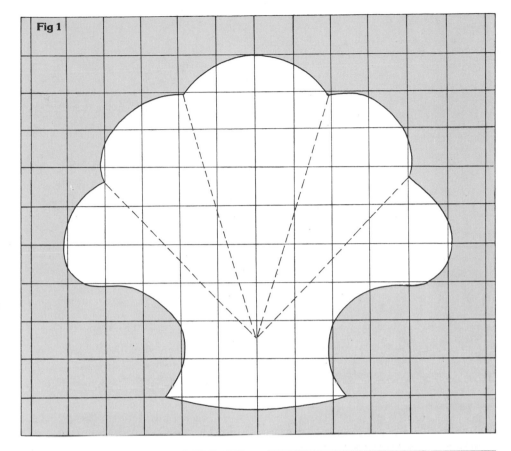

piping and pin, baste and stitch it to the right side of one cushion piece, following the instructions on page 10, Figs 5 and 6.

Lay the prepared frill on top of the piping, matching raw edges. Baste, using fairly small stitches (Fig 3). Lay the second cushion piece on top, matching edges. Baste, and then machine-stitch on the same stitching line as before, leaving a gap in the seam.

Turn the cushion to the right side and unpick the basting threads carefully. Insert the cushion pad and close the seam with slipstitches.

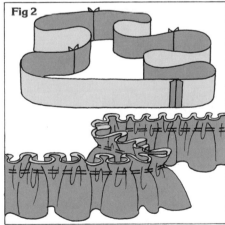

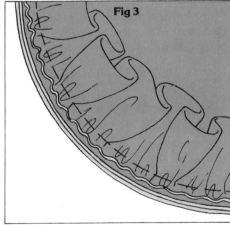

Fig 1 Graph pattern for the appliqué shell motif: scale 1 sq = 2.5cm (1in)

Fig 2 Making doubled frills: join strips of fabric end to end to make a ring. Fold along the length, gather the raw edges together

Fig 3 Applying a frill to fabric: baste the gathered frill to the right side of fabric, matching edges and sandwiching the piping. Apply lace or broderie trims in the same way

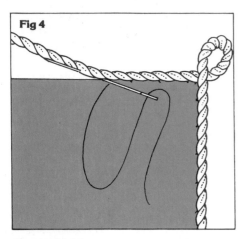
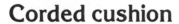

Fig 4 *Sew decorative cord to the cushion edges, taking the needle through 2 twists of the cord. Twist and stitch loops at corners*

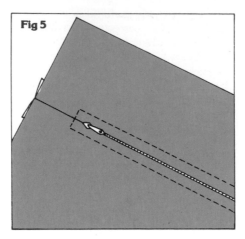

Fig 5 *Insert a zip into the back piece, one-quarter down from the top edge. Choose a zip 10cm (4in) shorter than the cushion width*

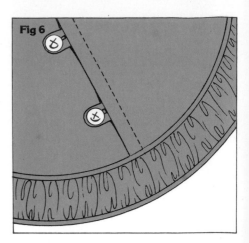

Fig 6 *Make round or square cushions with overlapping back sections, securing the opening with buttons and fabric loops*

Corded cushion

In the picture on pages 8–9, one square cushion has been edged with a silky cord. This is very simple to do and there are two ways of finishing the cord ends.

Preparation

Make up the cushion cover and insert the cushion pad. Close the seam with slipstitches, but leave a gap in the seam about 2.5cm (1in) long.

Measure round the cushion to estimate the quantity of cord required. Add 25cm (10in) to the measurement for corner loops and for joining ends.

Finishing

Begin at the open seam. Tuck the end of the cord into the opening and secure it to the seam allowances with a few small stitches. Sew the cord along the seam line, using small stitches and passing the needle between the twists of the cord (see Fig 4). At the corners, form the cord into a loop, stitching through the crossed cord to hold the shape.

Continue sewing the cord along the seam line. When the gap in the seam is reached, unpick the stitches holding the beginning of the cord in the opening. Cross the cord ends (see detail, Fig 4), and stitch the join. Complete the stitching of the cord to the cushion, closing the seam at the same time.

Tasselled corner For an alternative edging, start stitching the cord at a corner. Tie a tight knot in the cord about 10cm (4in) from the end. Sew the cord to the cushion as described.

When the corner is reached again, tie a knot in the cord end, and cut off any excess cord 10cm (4in) from the knot. Unravel and comb the cord ends to make tassels.

Gusseted cushion

A round cushion in the picture on pages 8–9 has a gathered gusset and piping set into the edges. This is a fairly complicated technique but you might like to try it. The finished effect, particularly if a satinised fabric or velvet is used, is very luxurious-looking.

Quick cushion cover

This cushion cover requires almost no sewing and the technique works best on a square cushion.

Measure one side of the cushion pad. Cut a square of fabric, the sides 1½ times the measurement, plus 2.5cm (1in). Neaten the edge with hand-sewing or machine-stitching. Sew ribbons or tapes to the corners. Lay the cushion pad on the fabric (see illustration) and tie the ribbons in the centre of the cushion.

Preparation

Cut the top and bottom pieces of the cushion cover. Measure round the cushion pad and cut the gusset to the depth desired plus 2.5cm (1in) seam allowance, and to a length twice the cushion's circumference.

Prepare and apply the piping as described on page 10, Figs 2–6.

Making the Cushion

Join the short ends of the gusset piece. Gather both long edges to the circumference of the cushion pieces. The gusset is applied and stitched to the cushion piece in the same way as for a frill (page 11, Fig 3), sandwiching the piping in between, but without leaving a gap in the seam.

The second cushion piece is prepared with piping and then stitched to the other edge of the gusset, with a gap left in the seam for inserting the cushion pad.

Zips and buttons

Zip fasteners are the most professional-looking closures for cushions but they can be a little tricky to insert into a piped seam. It is easier to insert the zip into the cushion back (see Fig 5). Cut the back piece 2.5cm (1in) deeper than the front piece. Cut across the width, about 10cm (4in) from one end.

Choose a zip fastener a little shorter than the width of the cushion back. Insert the zip between the cut edges of the fabric, centring it on the seam. Complete the seam at both ends of the zip (see Fig 5). Make up the cushion in the usual way.

Window dressing

Window curtains and drapes are the furnishings that homemakers most often want to sew for themselves. Windows come in a variety of shapes and sizes and it is not always possible to find ready-made curtains of the right dimensions. A new pair of curtains is also one of the quickest and most effective ways of brightening up or changing the look of a room. For a beginner, the easiest curtains are net curtains or unlined ones.

Net curtains

Nets, and sheer curtain fabrics, are available in several widths so you will probably be able to find a width which fits your particular window without having to join pieces. Also, as the selvedges are neat, there is no need to finish the side edges. Nets and sheers sometimes have decorative hems and the only sewing you have to do is to make a channel on the top edge for supporting wires or rods (see pages 14–15).

Unlined curtains

The best fabrics for unlined curtains are those with a fairly close weave so that the curtains do not stretch and sag after they are hung. It is also better to choose fabrics that look attractive from both sides. The curtains in the picture on page 13 are made from spotted cotton muslin and this type of fabric is not only easy to sew but the finished curtains will come up fresh and pretty even after countless launderings. However, as most fabrics suitable for curtains are only 120cm *(48in)* wide it is often necessary to join pieces on the side edges to get the width of fabric required. A straight seam is used for stitching widths together and, providing care is taken in matching the pattern, this need not present difficulties.

Hanging curtains

For curtains which will be kept permanently drawn across the window or, like those in the picture, are fastened back at the sides, an adjustable curtain rod or an expanding wire can be used. Rods are supported on square hooks screwed into the window frame at the sides (Fig 1a), while expanding wires have rings at the ends which fit onto hooks screwed into the frame (Fig 1b). Expanding wire is often used for hanging net curtains but it is not recommended for unlined curtains on windows wider than 135–150cm *(4½–5ft)* because the weight of the fabric causes the wire to sag in the middle.

For both rods and wires, a casing is made at the top of the curtain and the rod or wire is pushed through. The casing can be plain, as shown in the picture, or it can be made with a frill.

Estimating fabric

Fit the curtain rod or wire first. (If you are using an existing curtain track, the estimating procedure is the same.)

For short curtains, measure from the rod or wire to just above, or just below the window sill. For full-length curtains, measure to a point 2.5cm *(1in)* clear of the floor (Fig 2a).

If draped curtains are required, such as those in the picture, measure from the middle of the wire or rod, allowing the tape measure to curve, to the point on the wall where the curtains will be tied back, and then to the sill or to the floor (Fig 2b). Add 7.5cm *(3in)* to the measurement for the curtain heading. If a frill is required, add a further 5cm *(2in)*. For the bottom hem, allow 6cm *(2½in)*.

To estimate the total width of fabric required, measure the length of the rod, wire or curtain track. Net and sheer curtains look skimpy if they are not full enough so allow twice or even three times the measurement for each curtain. If an even greater width of net is required than is available, hang individual curtains side by side – the edges will be hidden in the folds.

For fabric curtains, allow at least double the width of the rod, wire or track for each curtain, 2½ times the

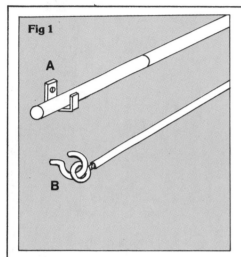

Fig 1

A

B

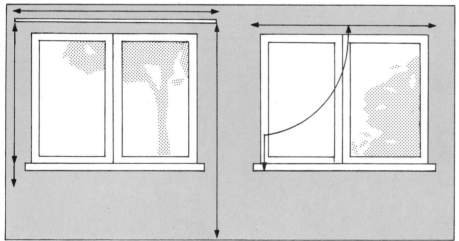

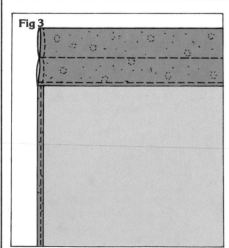

Fig 3

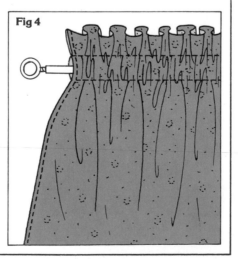

Fig 4

Fig 1 *Expanding rods fit onto square hooks screwed into the frame. Expanding wire has ring eyes screwed in the ends which slip over hooks screwed into the frame*

Fig 2A *Measure the width of the hanging system, then the depth to the window sill or to the floor*

Fig 2B *Allow the tape measure to hang in a curve to measure for draped curtains*

Fig 3 *Make a casing by working two rows of stitching along the curtain head*

Fig 4 *When the expanding wire or rod is inserted, the curtain is gathered along it*

width if the fabric is very light and soft.

Matching large patterns
If the fabric you are using has a large motif in the pattern, you should allow for this in estimating. You will probably need at least one extra pattern repeat on each length for matching the design (see page 16, Fig 1).

Making unlined curtains

Preparation
Measure and cut lengths of fabric carefully, cutting along threads in the weave to achieve straight edges. Press all creases from fabrics.

Match, pin, baste and stitch widths together to obtain the correct width of curtain if required. Press seams open.

Making up
Turn and iron a doubled 6mm (¼in) hem down both edges. Baste and machine-stitch close to the edge.

Turn and press a 12mm (½in) hem to the wrong side on the top edge. Turn another, 6cm (2½in) hem, press and baste. Machine-stitch close to the edge. This makes a plain casing and the rod or wire is pushed through from the open edges of the casing.

Frilled casing If a frill is required above the casing, measure the circumference of the curtain rod, or across the ring screw on the end of the expanding wire, to obtain the exact depth of casing required.

Mark the depth with pins then baste and machine-stitch across the curtain (see Fig 3). When the rod or wire is pushed into the casing and the curtain gathered up along its length, the fabric above the second row of stitching forms a frill (Fig 4).

Finishing
Slip the curtains onto the rod or wire and hang them to check the length. Pin up the hem. Take the curtains down and press along the fold of the hem.

Turn and press a narrow hem on the raw edge. Sew up the hem, using slip-stitches, or hemming, as you prefer. The hem can be machine-stitched but it should be done with closely matching thread so that the stitching hardly shows on the right side.

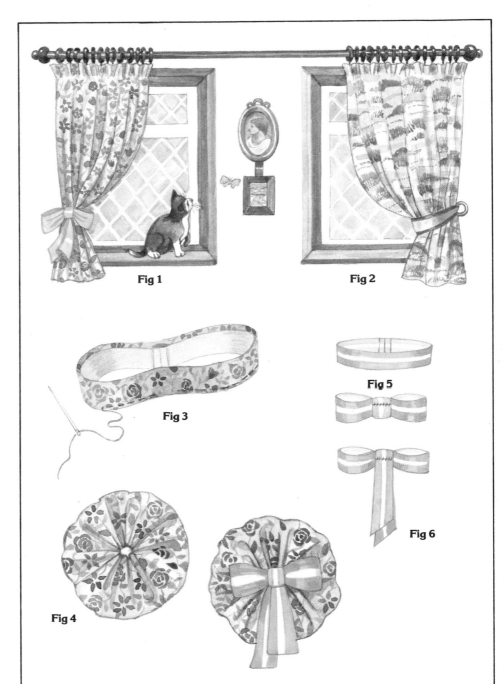

Fig 1

Fig 2

Fig 3

Fig 5

Fig 6

Fig 4

Tie-backs
Curtain tie-backs can be made from a length of ribbon or braid, tied in a bow. For a simpler effect, slip a piece of wide ribbon onto a curtain ring and stitch the ends. Hang the ring over a hook screwed into the window frame or wall (Figs 1 and 2).

The picture shows rosettes of the curtain fabric trimmed with striped ribbon bows used for tie-backs. To make these, cut a strip of fabric 90 × 6cm (36 × 2½in) for each rosette. Join the short ends of a strip and stitch a narrow hem along one edge (Fig 3). Run

gathering stitches along the other edge and pull up the thread to form the rosette. Finish with two or three stitches in the centre (Fig 4).

For each ribbon bow, cut a piece of 25mm (1in)-wide ribbon 23cm (9in) long. Stitch the ends together. Flatten the ribbon circle into a bow (Fig 5). Cut a piece of ribbon 8cm (3¼in) long. Wrap and sew the piece round the middle of the bow to make a 'waist'. Fold a 30cm (12in) length of ribbon and sew to the back of the bow for 'tails' (Fig 6). Sew the bow to the rosette. Sew tape or ribbon ties to the back of the rosettes to tie the curtains.

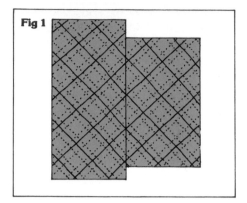

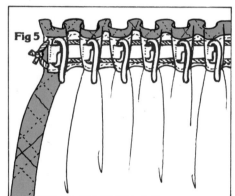

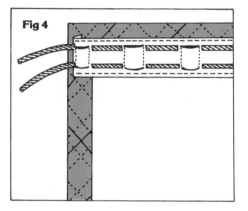

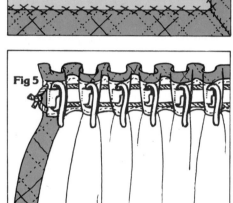

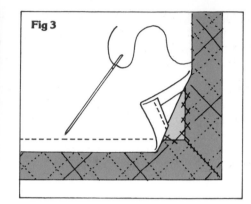

Fig 1 *Allow at least one extra repeat on each curtain length for matching the pattern*

Fig 2 *Turn the curtain hems to the wrong side and Herringbone-stitch, mitring the bottom corners*

Fig 3 *Fold and press the lining side hems and machine-stitch the bottom hem. Slipstitch to the curtain*

Fig 4 *Machine-stitch the tape along both edges and across the ends*

Fig 5 *Pull up the tape cords to the desired curtain width. Knot the cord ends.*

Lined curtains

Full-length lined curtains add dramatic emphasis to a room by bringing in colour, texture and pattern. They are a simple project, even for a beginner and what is needed more than sewing skill is a large flat area to work on. A large table, with the length of fabric supported on chair backs is ideal, otherwise, use the floor.

The lining is hand-sewn to the curtain and this is not as slow nor as difficult as it sounds. When large amounts of fabric are involved, hand-sewing is often easier than using a sewing machine.

The curtains in the picture have a deep, pencil pleat heading which looks particularly effective when used with a curtain pole and rings.

Estimating fabric

Before measuring, fix the pole or curtain track in position.

From the pole or track, measure down to where the curtain hem is to be. With full-length curtains, the hem should just clear the floor. Add 10cm (4in) for the bottom hem and 12mm (½in) on the top edge.

The type of heading tape you choose will, to an extent, determine the width of fabric required. For a pencil-pleat heading, such as that used for the curtains pictured, each curtain requires fabric 2½ times the window width.

To estimate the amount of fabric needed, work out how many widths of your fabric need to be joined to achieve the measurement. Large-scale patterns must be accurately matched on the edges and for this, you should allow one extra repeat on every curtain length. (Fig 1.)

Allow 5cm (2in) for the side seams and 15mm (⅝in) for any seams needed to join widths. If the curtains are to overlap in the middle, allow an extra 15cm (6in) to the width of both curtains.

You will need the same amount of lining fabric.

You will also need sufficient pleating tape for the full width of both curtains, plus 5cm (2in) on each piece.

Preparation

Cut the fabric into lengths, taking care to cut ends square with the edges. Cut off the selvedges. Cut the lining fabric to the same lengths.

Making the curtains

Spread the fabric lengths, wrong side up and pin the edges together, matching the pattern. Baste, removing the pins. Machine-stitch the seam, taking a 15mm (⅝in) seam allowance. Machine-stitch in the same direction on each joining seam – it helps to prevent distortion when the curtains are hung. Press the seam flat, then open. Work all the seams in the same way. Join the lining lengths in the same way.

Spread the curtain flat, wrong side up. Turn a narrow hem down both long edges, then turn the full 5cm (2in) hem. Baste, then sew with Herringbone Stitch (Fig 2). Turn up the bottom edge, mitring the corners neatly, and slipstitch (refer to page 7, Fig 3 for mitring technique).

Lining

Spread the lining flat on the curtain, wrong sides facing, matching edges. On the lining, measure and then cut 4cm (1½in) from both long edges and from the bottom edge. Turn a narrow hem to the wrong side on the bottom edge, then turn and baste a second hem, so that the lining is approximately 2.5cm (1in) shorter than the curtain. Machine-stitch the lining hem. Press.

Spread the lining on the curtain again, wrong sides facing and matching the top edges. Pin the top edges, smoothing the lining on the curtain.

Turn the side edges of the lining

under, pinning them to the curtain, so that about 2.5cm *(1in)* of the curtain shows. Slip-stitch the lining to the curtain down both edges (Fig 3).

Attaching the heading

On the top edge, remove the pins and turn both fabrics 12mm *(¹/₂in)* to the wrong side. Pin.

Unpick the last 5cm *(2in)* of the heading tape cords. Turning the end of the tape under, pin the tape along the top of the curtain on the wrong side, close to the edge. Re-thread the cords and knot them together.

At the other end of the curtain, unpick the cords for about 5cm *(2in)*, measure and cut the tape leaving 2.5cm *(1in)* for turning. Turn the tape end under. Re-thread the cords and knot together loosely.

Machine-stitch along both long sides of the tape and across the ends, taking care not to catch in the cords (Fig 4). Remove basting. Untie the knotted cords at one end and pull up the pencil pleats evenly. Knot the cord ends but do not cut them. Work the other curtain the same way, making sure that the curtain is pulled up from the outside edge. The knotted cord ends will lie at the middle of the window. Insert the hooks (Fig 5).

Chair seat cover

Chairs with drop-in seats are simple to re-cover when they become worn, or when a quick change is required to brighten up a room.

If the seat has sagged, the webbing has probably worn and the chair needs re-upholstering but if the webbing seems tight, you need only replace the wadding before putting on the new cover fabric.

Estimating fabric

Remove the chair seat and measure the existing area of fabric, adding 5cm (2in) to both the width and the length measurements. Measure the 'scrim' on the seat back. Add 5cm (2in) all round.

Materials required

Furnishing fabric as estimated
Cotton or polyester wadding
Black 'scrim' fabric for backing as estimated
Plastic wood filler
Box of upholsterer's large-headed 12mm (1/2in) tacks

Tools required

Chisel (old, with blunt edge), mallet, tack hammer

Preparation

Using the mallet and chisel to lift out the tacks, remove the backing scrim, then remove the old fabric. Lift off the old wadding to expose the hessian underneath. Fill the tack holes with plastic wood filler.

Measure and mark the middle point on all four sides of the fabric. Mark the seat frame in the same way.

Cut a piece of wadding a little larger than the seat so that it falls short of the bottom edges on all four sides (Fig 1).

Covering the seat

Spread the cover fabric over the wadding matching the marked points on the fabric and the chair seat frame. Pin the fabric to the wadding so that you can turn the seat over and work from the back. Remove the pins.

Bring the fabric up onto the seat frame on the back edge and tap one tack into the middle of the side (Fig 2).

Pull the fabric gently at the front edge and bring it over onto the seat frame. Tap in a tack to hold the fabric temporarily in the middle of the side. From the tack on the back edge, tap in more tacks working towards the back corners. Tacks should be about 2cm (3/4in) in from the edge and approximately 3cm (1 1/4in) apart.

Now stretch the fabric onto the frame on the right and tap in one holding tack as before. Pull up the fabric on the left side, stretching it smoothly and tap in one holding tack.

Tap in tacks each side of the holding tacks, working towards the corners, and keeping the fabric as smooth and as taut as possible.

Finally, remove the front edge holding tack and pull the fabric up and onto the frame so that it is smooth and quite taut. Tack the fabric to the frame, setting the first tack in the middle again and then working towards the corners.

Corners Following Fig 3, fold the corners of the cover onto the frame. Tack, then cut off the corner points. Cut the fabric away under the folded edges to reduce bulk. Fold the fabric onto the frame and complete the tacking as shown in Fig 4.

Attaching the scrim

Check to see that all the tacks are hammered home and lie flush with the surface of the wood.

Lay the scrim on the back of the chair seat and trim the edges to the shape, leaving approximately 2.5cm (1in) for turnings. Lay the bottom edge of the scrim on the bottom edge of the frame, right side down and tack to the seat. Fold the scrim up onto the frame and turn the top edge under. Tack across. Fold the side edges under and complete tacking the scrim.

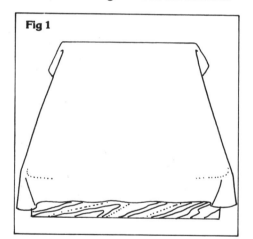

Fig 1 *Cut a piece of wadding so that it is a little larger than the chair seat*

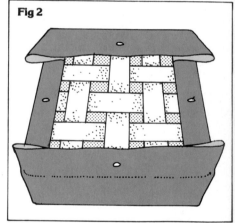

Fig 2 *Fold the fabric onto the front and back edges, setting holding tacks, then set more tacks, working towards the corners*

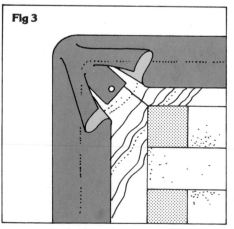

Fig 3 *Fold the corner onto the seat frame and hold with one tack. Trim away the excess fabric*

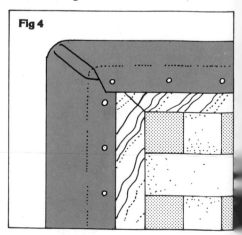

Fig 4 *Fold the side edges towards the corner and then complete the tacking*

Slip cover for an armchair

New slip covers on armchairs can transform the look of a room immediately. Summer slip covers can be made in light-coloured fabrics, with a change of looks in winter with different fabrics. When a decorative scheme is being planned, new slip covers can bring both colour and pattern into the room.

For your first attempt, work with a small chair that has a simple shape.

Estimating fabric

The illustration, Fig 1, identifies the various parts and surfaces of an armchair. Each section is measured separately as a square or rectangular piece of fabric. The Inside Back, for instance, is measured from top to bottom, A–A, and then across the width, B–B. Measure each section in this way and note the dimensions.

Fig 2 shows how each section looks in fabric. Draw a similar chart for yourself on squared paper, identifying each section as it is measured. Very approximately, a slip cover for an armchair of average size takes between 5 and 7 metres (5½–8 yards) of fabric.

Allow an extra metre (yard) for cutting bias strips for piping. This can either be in the main fabric colour or a contrasting fabric can be used. As you measure the sections, add a 3cm (1⅛in) seam allowance on all four sides.

The seams of the Inside Back, Inside Arms and Seat are tucked down into the chair when the slip cover is on. On

these edges, add an extra 10cm (4in) for tuck-in.

If the chair has loose cushions, measure these also. As the various sections are drawn on the chart remember that the fabric pattern must run in the same direction on all sections (see Fig 2).

The armchair in the picture has been covered with a striped fabric and this is a good choice for a first project. A regular stripe makes it simple to cut straight edges, and it is also easier to centre sections on the chair.

Piping has been inserted on the front edges and round the loose cushion. A plainer, boxy shape without cushions would be piped along most of the seams.

Measure the chair and any cushions for the total length of piping cord required, allowing approximately 45cm (18in) for joining ends.

Preparation

Pre-shrink the piping cord if it is made of cotton (see page 8, Square piped cushion).

Cut bias strips of fabric and cover the piping cord (see page 10). Measure and cut out the sections, identifying each

Fig 1 *Each section of the chair is measured across the widest and deepest points. Fabric is cut in square or rectangular pieces*

Fig 2 *As each section is measured, add the seam allowance and draw the shape on squared paper to make a fabric layout*

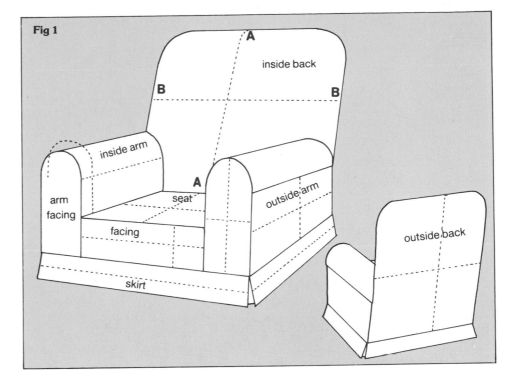

Fig 1

inside back

B   B

inside arm

A

arm facing

seat

outside arm

facing

outside back

skirt

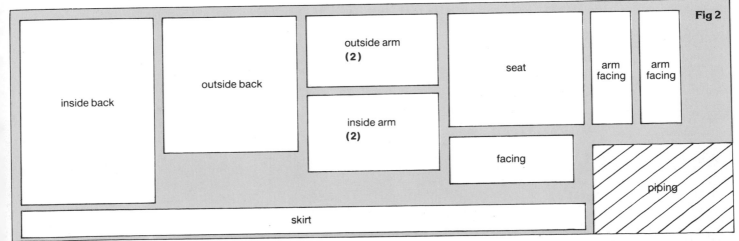

Fig 2

inside back

outside back

outside arm (2)

inside arm (2)

seat

arm facing

arm facing

facing

piping

skirt

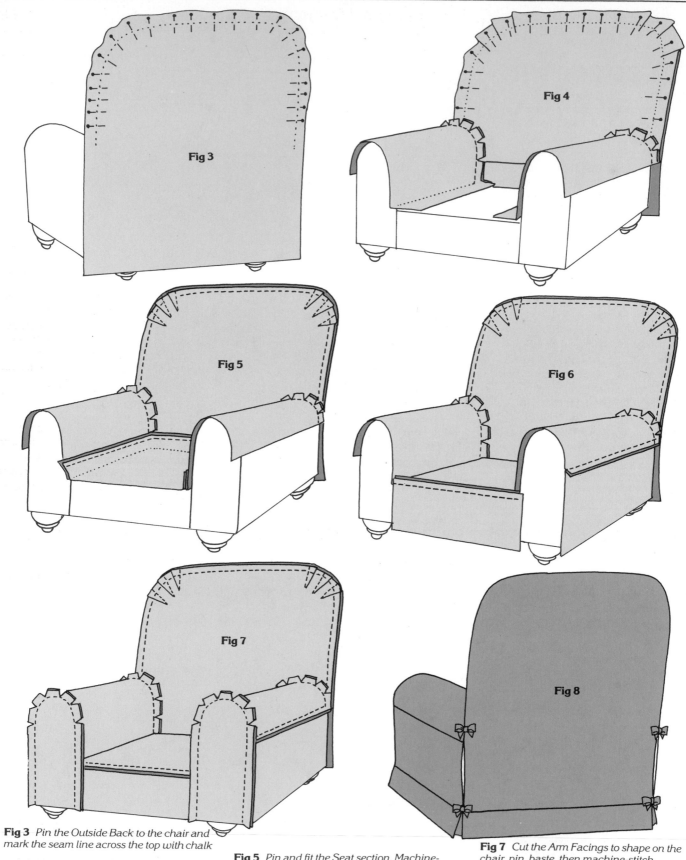

Fig 3 Pin the Outside Back to the chair and mark the seam line across the top with chalk

Fig 4 Pin the Inside Back to the Outside Back, pleating and pinning the fabric to follow the chair's curved top. Cut the fabric where it meets the Inside Arm sections, clipping into the fabric edges for ease. Fold back the tuck-in allowances

Fig 5 Pin and fit the Seat section. Machine-stitch the tuck-in allowance edges to the Inside Back and Inside Arm section

Fig 6 Tuck-ins tucked into the seat sides. Pin and stitch the Facing to the Seat, then attach the Outside Arms to the Inside Arms

Fig 7 Cut the Arm Facings to shape on the chair, pin, baste, then machine-stitch, clipping into the seam allowances for ease

Fig 8 Neaten the Outside Back and Outside Arm edges where they meet at the chair corners with narrow machine-stitched seams. Sew on ties for fastening the cover

piece with dressmaker's chalk or pencil on the wrong side.

Using chalk, measure and mark the vertical centre on the Outside Back of the chair. Mark the Outside Back fabric in the same way.

Making the slip cover

Setting pins vertically, pin the Outside Back section to the chair, right side of the fabric to the chair (see Fig 3). Draw a chalk line across the top where the seam will fall.

Fit the Inside Back section to the chair and pin to the Outside Back on the top edge of the chair, pinning tiny pleats to take up the fullness (see Fig 4). Smooth the fabric to the chair's shape. Over the arms, cut the fabric to shape leaving a 3cm (1⅛in) seam allowance. Clip into the curves to ease the fabric so that it follows the contours of the chair.

Pin the Inside Arm sections next, cutting the fabric to follow the shape of the arms and leaving a seam allowance.

Clip into the seam allowance, and pin the seam allowances of the Inside Arm and Inside Back together (Fig 4).

At this stage, remove the slip cover from the chair and baste the pinned seams. Remove the pins and machine-stitch the seams. Put the slip cover back on the chair.

Seat section

Following Fig 5, fit the Seat section, remembering that it has tuck-in allowances on three sides. Pin the edges of the Seat's tuck-in allowances to the edges of the Inside Back and Inside Arm allowances. These can be basted while the slip cover is on the chair.

Pin the Seat Facing section to the front edge of the Seat section, inserting the prepared piping between.

Remove the slip cover and baste the Seat Facing-Seat seam. Machine-stitch the seam, and also the tuck-in allowance seams. Put the slip cover back on the chair, and push the tuck-ins down the sides of the seat (Fig 6). Pin the Outside Arm sections to the Inside Arm sections. Baste and machine-stitch (Fig 6). The seam between the Outside Arm and the Back section is left open.

Pin the Arm Facing sections to the slip cover, inserting the prepared piping between the edges. Cut the top edge in

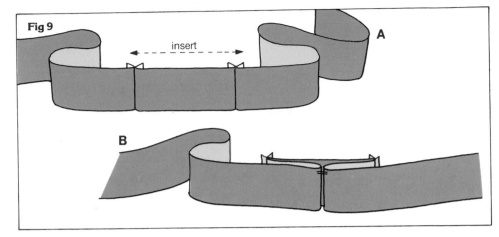

Fig 9 *Make the Skirt section so that the inverted pleat inserts are at the four corners of the chair. Press and catch the pleats, and attach the Skirt to the cover*

a curve to follow the chair's contours, leaving a seam allowance. Clip into the seam allowance to ease the curve. Remove the slip cover from the chair, baste and machine-stitch the seams.

Making the skirt

The Skirt is in one piece from a Back corner, round the Front and to the other Back corner, with an inverted pleat at the front corners. The Back Skirt section is separate. Make the Skirt, inserting short pieces where the inverted pleats are to be. Machine-stitch the joins and press the seams open (Fig 9a). Machine-stitch a hem on the lower edge. Fold the inverted pleat and press

(Fig 9b). Baste. Neaten the short ends of the Skirt. Pin and baste the Skirt to the slip cover's lower edge, right sides of fabric facing. Machine stitch. Make the Back Skirt to the same depth. Neaten the short ends and stitch to the slip cover.

Finishing

Neaten the edges of the open seam between the Outside Back and Outside Arm. Make ties from fabric and sew to the edges to tie and close the slip cover (Fig 8). Turn the cover to the right side and give it a final press.

Cushions

Cover any cushions, inserting the prepared piping, following the instructions for Garden box cushions on page 60.

Slip-over chair cover

Once you have learned how to make a fitted slip cover for an armchair the techniques can be adapted to making slip-over covers for small armless chairs.

Use ready-quilted fabric for the chair back and seat or, if you prefer, baste the fabric to thin wadding and then cut and stitch the fabrics as one.

Make a paper pattern of the chair back

and the seat. Cut two backs and one seat adding seam allowances. Cut a frill twice the circumference of the chair seat and to the measurement from the seat to the floor.

Stitch the back pieces together leaving the bottom edge open. Stitch the bottom edge of the inside back to the back edge of the seat. Gather the frill piece to fit the seat and stitch to the seat and the bottom edge of the outside chair back.

Pleated lampshade

Even if you have not attempted lampshade making before, you will find the method used to make this pleated lampshade simple and successful. The lampshade is not lined but instructions for making linings are on page 26, should you want to try this refinement to the design. Once you have learned to make a lining, you will be able to make classic lampshades of every shape.

Estimating fabric

Measure the depth of the shade from the top to the bottom ring. Add 7.5cm (3in) to the measurement.

Measure round the bottom ring and allow three times the circumference. These two measurements give you the dimensions of fabric required.

Materials required

Strutted lampshade frame
White cotton binding tape
Soft, lightweight fabric
Matching sewing thread
All-purpose adhesive

Preparation

The top and bottom rings of the frame are covered with binding tape. Knot the tape end loosely round a strut on the top ring. Wind the tape smoothly and tightly over the ring. When the next strut is reached, twist the tape in a figure-of-eight (see Fig 1) and continue winding.

Work all the struts in the same way. To finish, untie the knot and glue the tape ends together. Cover the bottom ring in the same way.

Making the lampshade

Turn 1cm (⅜in) on one short end of the fabric to the wrong side. Align the fold with a strut, with approximately 4cm (1½in) of fabric extending above the frame. Insert a pin vertically through the fold, pinning the fabric to the top ring. Working to the left, fold the next pleat and pin Fig 2). The pleats are made on the straight grain of fabric and should be evenly spaced.

When the next strut is reached, insert the last pin in the top ring, then start pleating the bottom edge. These pleats will be more widely spaced. Insert pins vertically, pinning the fabric to the bottom ring (Fig 3).

Continue in the same way, pleating on the top ring and the bottom ring alternately.

When all the pleats are formed and pinned, tuck the fabric end under the edge of the first pleat made. (This technique is also used to join in separate pieces of fabric while pleating.)

Oversew the fabric to the rings, using small stitches (see Fig 4). Trim away the excess fabric above the top ring and below the bottom ring.

Finishing

Finish the lampshade by covering the top and bottom rings with bias-cut strips of fabric, sewing the binding to the fabric with tiny stitches on both the inside and the outside of the shade (Fig 5). Remove the pins as you sew.

Turn the ends under and hem the edges together neatly.

The bias binding can also be glued round the rings but this must be carefully done, using only a little adhesive, so that none seeps through the fabric to the right side.

Ready-made bias binding can also be used, or other kinds of lampshade trimming, such as braid, can be applied.

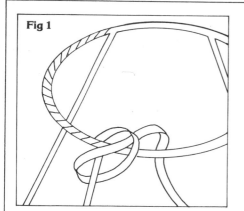

Fig 1

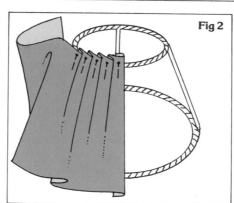

Fig 2

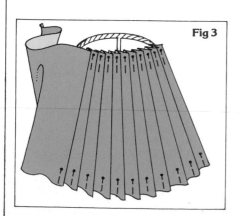

Fig 3

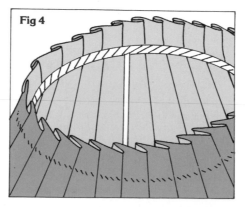

Fig 4

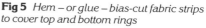

Fig 1 *Tape the top and bottom rings. When struts are reached, wind the tape in a figure-of-eight. Continue taping. Glue the end*

Fig 2 *Fold 9mm (⅜in) under on the short end of fabric. Pin to the top ring. Pleat, overlapping pleats to the first strut*

Fig 3 *At struts, pin pleats to the bottom ring, pulling the fabric taut. Pleats will be more widely spaced*

Fig 4 *Work small hemming stitches through the pleats, sewing fabric to the rings. Cut away excess fabric*

Fig 5 *Hem – or glue – bias-cut fabric strips to cover top and bottom rings*

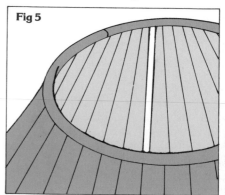

Fig 5

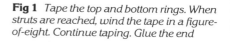

Making a lining

A lining is made and put on the frame before the outer shade is made. First, cover the frame's struts and top and bottom rings with binding tape.

Estimating fabric

Measure the depth of the frame and add 7.5cm (3in) to the measurement. Measure round the bottom ring and add 15cm (6in) to the measurement. These two measurements give the fabric dimensions.

Preparation

Cut the fabric down the middle to give two pieces of the same size. Temporarily pin the pieces together, right sides facing, matching raw edges.

Making the lining

Lay the frame on a flat surface. Arrange

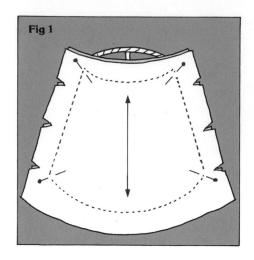

Fig 1

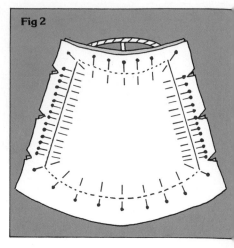

Fig 2

the doubled fabric over the frame. Pin the fabric to the points where the side struts meet the top and bottom rings (see Fig 1). Remove the temporary pins. Gently stretching the doubled fabric, insert pins in the middle of the side struts, taking the pins through the fabric into the binding tape. The pin points should lie inwards, to avoid unnecessary scratches on your hands.

Insert more pins, closely spaced, on each side of the first pin, working towards the top and bottom rings. As you pin, pull the fabric so that it lies smoothly stretched across the frame. Clip into the fabric edges.

Next, insert a few pins along the top and bottom rings, stretching the fabric smoothly (see Fig 2).

Using a sharply-pointed soft pencil,

Quick lampshades

Bloomsbury shade

Tiffany shade

Lace shade

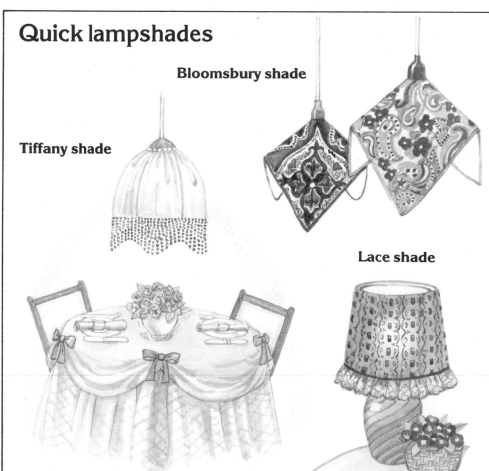

Sometimes, a quick change is required for a lampshade. Perhaps the existing cover has become soiled or torn, or a different colour scheme may be required

Bloomsbury shade

Large handkerchiefs or square scarves make a Bloomsbury shade. Cut a small circle of iron-on interfacing and press it to the middle of the fabric on the wrong side. Cut a circular hole through the interfacing and fabric. Drape the fabric over a coolie shade, and slip the shade onto the fitting. Use a low-watt bulb.

Tiffany shade

Make a pretty lace cover for a Tiffany-shaped shade. Choose lace with a scalloped edge, or sew on an edging. Join the short ends of a strip, making a casing on the top edge and insert elastic or a length of narrow ribbon. Pull up the gathers and fit over the shade. Tiffany shades can also be made of plain, silky fabrics and the edge might be trimmed with fringing.

Lace shade

Wide lace insertion makes a pretty bedroom lampshade. Cut lengths of lace twice the depth of a drum-shaped frame, plus 2.5cm (1in) for joining. Wind the lace over the frame and glue the overlapped ends together on the inside. The strips of lace should just touch.

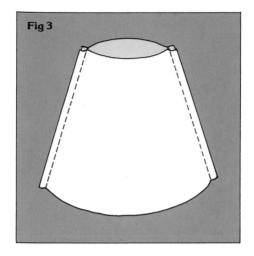

Fig 3

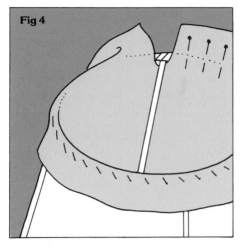

Fig 4

Fig 1 *Pin lining pieces, right sides facing, at corners, with the straight grain vertical to the frame*

Fig 2 *Stretch fabric smoothly, inserting pins through side struts. Continue pinning, setting pins each side. Pencil a line along the side struts*

Fig 3 *Stitch along the pencilled lines and trim back the seam allowances to 6mm (¹/₄in)*

Fig 4 *Slip the lining on the shade. Pin to top and bottom rings, then hem. Cut away excess fabric, snipping at gimbles*

mark the fabric along the side struts.

Pin the fabric layers together round the outside edges and then unpin the fabric from the frame. Baste along the marked lines, then machine-stitch. Unpick the basting and trim the seam (Fig 3). Put the lining into the frame, wrong side to the frame and matching the seams with side struts. Pin at top and bottom. Turn the excess fabric over the rings and pin all round, setting the pins as shown in Fig 4. Snip into the fabric edge at the gimbles.

Oversew the lining to the bound rings, using small stitches and keeping the lining stretched and smooth. Trim the excess fabric close to the stitching.

Making a classic lampshade
The same technique is used when making a cover for a classically-shaped frame. Make and insert the lining first. Make the outer cover and put it on the frame, right side out. Oversew the fabric to the top and bottom rings, as for the lining, and trim away the excess fabric. The stitching is covered when the bias binding is applied.

Drum shade
Some roller blind fabrics are already stiffened and can be used to cover drum-shaped frames. Glue the fabric to the top and bottom rings overlapping the long edges, holding it to the frame with clothes pins while the glue dries. Cover the top and bottom edges with braid, glueing it to the fabric.

Skirt shade
Soft, fabric shades can also be fitted over an existing lampshade. Join the short ends of a strip. Turn a 5cm *(2in)* hem on the top edge, then make a casing about 2.5cm *(1in)* from the edge. Insert narrow ribbon and draw up the top edge to fit the top of the lampshade. Tie the ribbon ends in a bow. Finish the bottom edge with a hem. Use a pretty, lightweight fabric such as spotted muslin. Slip the fabric skirt over the lampshade.

Ribbon shade
Remove the fabric from an old lampshade. Paint the frame with white gloss paint if necessary, or choose a pastel colour. Wind inexpensive gift ribbon over the top and bottom rings, overlapping the edges of the ribbon. Finish by glueing ribbon ends together. For a different look, gather two or three ribbons together at intervals with narrow ribbons, tied in bows.

Drum shade

Skirt shade

Ribbon shade

Bedrooms

By nature of their use, bed sheets, duvets and quilts involve considerable amounts of fabric but do not let this deter you. The construction techniques are very simple. Begin with this pretty quilt-comforter, tied with bright ribbons

Ribboned quilt

Lightweight interlining makes this quilt warm and comforting and the small ribbon bows look decorative and fun. Make sure that both fabrics and ribbons are machine-washable.

Materials required

For a quilt to fit a single size bed
254 × 160cm *(100 × 63in)* cotton or cotton/polyester fabric
218 × 124cm *(86 × 49in)* soft cotton curtain interlining
177 × 87cm *(69½ × 34in)* polyester wadding, 3cm *(1¼in)* thick
180 × 90cm *(71 × 36in)* backing fabric
1m *(1⅛yd)* each of 1cm *(⅜in)*-wide polyester satin ribbons in the following colours: mauve, yellow, pink, blue, green and orange
Matching sewing threads

Preparation

Make sure that all fabric pieces, interlining and wadding are cut square at the corners.

Making the quilt

On the main quilt piece, turn and press a 17cm *(7in)* border to the wrong side on all four sides. Turn under a further 12mm *(½in)* and mitre the corners of the quilt (see page 7, Fig 3).

Spread the soft cotton interlining on the wrong side of the quilt, under the turned border.

Spread the polyester wadding on the soft interfacing. Pin and then baste all round the edges of the quilt to hold the wadding in place.

Press a 15mm *(⅝in)* turning to the wrong side on all four sides of the backing fabric. Spread it right side up on the polyester wadding.

Sew the backing to the quilt border with slipstitches or with hemming. Remove the basting threads.

On the top side of the quilt, measure and baste a line 16cm *(6½in)* from the edges. Set the machine to a large stitch and machine-stitch along the basted line, pivoting the needle at the corners. (Roll up the quilt so that its bulk fits under the sewing machine's arm for stitching.) Work a second row of machine-stitching 6mm *(¼in)* outside the first row.

Ribbon bows

The diagram (Fig 1) shows the position of the coloured ribbon bows. The bows are set approximately 23cm *(9in)* in from the stitched border and the same distance apart horizontally. The bows are slightly closer together vertically.

Mark the positions for the bows on the quilt with basting or with chalk.

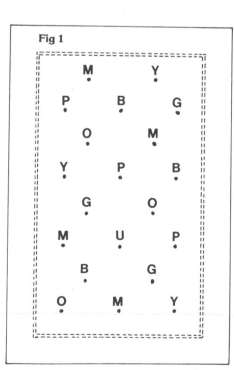

Fig 1 *Position the ribbon bows 22.5cm (9in) apart horizontally and the same distance from the double-stitched border. Bows are set slightly closer vertically. Follow the key: M–Mauve, Y–Yellow, P–Pink, B–Blue, G–Green, O–Orange*

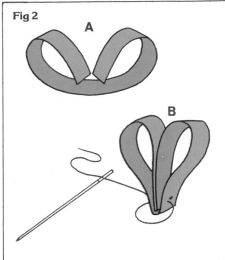

Fig 2 *Making stitched bows: bring the ribbon ends to the middle. Pinch the middle together and sew 2 or 3 stitches to hold the bow*

Cut pieces of ribbon 24cm *(9¹/₂in)* long. Fold the ends to the middle (Fig 2a). Pinch the middle of the bow and sew a few stitches through the thicknesses to hold the bow together (Fig 2b). Using the same thread, sew each bow in place through all thicknesses of the quilt, securing the thread ends neatly on the wrong side.

Ribbon quilting
For a different effect, thread a large-eyed, sharp needle with 1.5mm *(¹/₁₆in)*-wide ribbon. Take the needle from the top side of the quilt, through all thicknesses, then back up again from the under side about 3mm *(¹/₈in)* away. Cut the ribbon and tie the ends in a double knot, then a bow. The same quilting technique can be worked using 3mm *(¹/₈in)*-wide satin ribbon.

Ribbon pillows

Pillow covers can be made to match the quilt but instead of ribbon bows, which might produce a fussy effect, machine-stitch 12mm *(¹/₂in)*-wide satin ribbons across the cover in a trellis effect. A single or double ribbon bow might be stitched to one corner.

A nightdress or pyjama case, appliquéd with ribbons in the same colour scheme is another pretty accessory idea. To do this, pin and baste the ribbons diagonally across the top case piece, then machine-stitch along both edges. Make the case as for a cushion.

Beautiful bed linen

Bed sheets, pillowcases and duvet covers are well worth making at home, particularly if you are planning a co-ordinated colour scheme. Sheeting can be bought in wide widths and in a variety of plain colours and patterns to suit every kind of furnishing mood.

Materials required

For a standard double bed, 1 bottom sheet, 1 duvet cover, 2 Oxford pillowcases

2.75m *(3yd)* of 2.30m *(90in)*-wide sheeting (sheet)

4.10m *(4½yd)* of 2.30m *(90in)*-wide sheeting, duvet cover

1.50m *(1⅝yd)* of fastener tape (duvet)

2.40m *(2⅝yd)* of 2.75m *(108in)*-wide sheeting (pillowcases)

Matching sewing threads

Preparation

For the sheet, cut the fabric ends square to the selvedges. For the duvet cover, cut the fabric to 2.05m (81in) wide. For each pillowcase, cut one piece 107 × 60cm *(42 × 24in)* and one piece 83 × 60cm *(32 × 24in)*.

Making the sheet

At the bottom end of the sheet fold a 2cm *(¾in)* double hem to the wrong side. Press, baste and machine-stitch.

Turn a narrow hem to the wrong side on the top edge, then fold and press a 5cm *(2in)* hem. Baste and machine-stitch close to the edge. Work a second row of stitching 6mm *(1/4in)* away.

Making the duvet cover

Fold the fabric in half across. The folded edge is the top edge. On the bottom edges, turn double 2.5cm *(1in)* hems to the inside for the duvet opening. Pin, baste and then machine-stitch. Mark the middle of the opening with a pin. With right sides together and the hems matching, machine-stitch along the fold of the hems from the sides towards the middle, stopping stitching 75cm *(30in)* from the pin marker. This leaves an opening 152cm *(60in)* wide.

Inserting the fastener tape Machine-stitch the tape into the opening using a zipper foot on the machine. Stitch along both edges of the tape.

Turn the duvet cover right sides out and machine-stitch across the hem ends to enclose the raw ends (Fig 1).

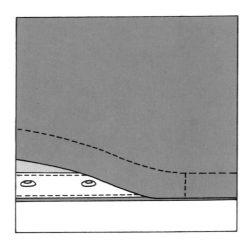

Fig 1 *Machine-stitch the tape along both edges inside the duvet opening. Machine-stitch across the opening ends to secure the tape ends*

Finishing

Finish the sides of the duvet cover with french seams.

If preferred, fabric ties or ribbons can be stitched along the opening instead of fastener tape. Five pairs of ties would be needed for a 152cm *(60in)* opening. (Refer to page 53, Fig 4 for making fabric ties.)

Making a pillowcase

On both pieces, make a narrow hem on one short end to the wrong side 1cm *(3/8in)* wide (Figs 2a and 2b). The larger piece is the front of the pillowcase.

On the front piece, fold the hemmed edge to the right side of fabric 18cm *(7 1/4in)*. From the fold, machine-stitch 5cm *(2in)* on both edges (Fig 2c).

Turn the fold to the wrong side and press.

With wrong sides facing, lay the smaller piece on the larger, matching the raw edges and tucking the hemmed edge under the fold (Fig 2d).

Pin, baste and machine-stitch on three sides (see Fig 2d), taking a 6mm *(1/4in)* seam.

Turn the pillowcase wrong side out and complete the french seam (see page 64). Press firmly.

Mark a line 5cm *(2in)* in from the edges on the front of the pillowcase. Work over the line with a wide machine satin stitch, making sure that the pillowcase opening is not caught into the stitching (see Fig 2e).

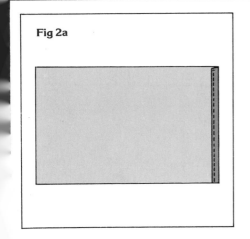

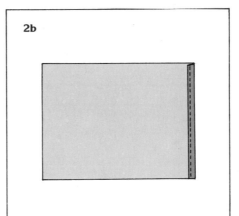

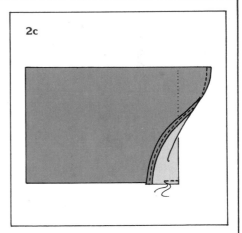

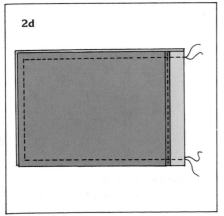

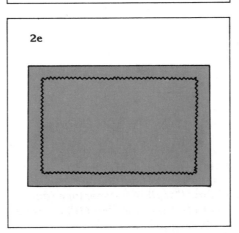

Fig 2a *Make a narrow doubled hem on one short end of the pillowcase front piece*

2b *Make a narrow doubled hem on one short end of the pillowcase back piece*

2c *Fold down 18cm (7in) on the hemmed end. Machine-stitch 5cm (2in) on both edges, from the fold*

2d *Lay the back piece on the front piece, matching edges, wrong sides facing and machine-stitch on three sides*

2e *Work a border of machine satin stitch on the pillowcase front*

Buttoned headboard

The headboard pictured is based on a shape sometimes found on French beds. Tall and impressive it will add character to any bedroom.

The method used to make the headboard is quick to do and not at all difficult, but a heavy-duty staple gun is an essential piece of equipment. No special upholstery skills are needed. Black and white ticking fabric and bright red rope trim have been used for the headboard in the picture but the techniques can be used with other fabrics and trims.

Materials required

150 × 135cm *(60 × 53in)* piece of 2cm *(³/₄in)*-thick chipboard
150 × 135cm *(60 × 53in)* piece of 6cm *(2¹/₂in)*-thick wadding
107 × 60cm *(42 × 24in)* piece of 6cm *(2¹/₂in)*-thick polyester wadding
1.70m *(1⁷/₈yd)* of 1.40m *(1¹/₂yd)*-wide furnishing fabric
1.70m *(1⁷/₈yd)* of furnishing scrim
3m *(3¹/₄yd)* thick, soft, red rope
15 buttons or button moulds
12mm *(¹/₂in)* tacks
Fabric adhesive
Strong button thread and curved upholstery needle
Heavy-duty staple gun

Preparation

Tape sheets of newspaper together for pattern paper. From Fig 1, draw a grid of squares (scale 1 sq – 10cm *(4in)*) and draw the shape of the headboard to size. Mark the positions of the buttons on the paper pattern.

Use the pattern to cut the chipboard to shape.

If button moulds are being used, cover them with fabric.

Making the headboard

Spread the larger piece of wadding on the hardboard and staple it to the front of the board, working close to the edge. Trim away the excess wadding on the top curve.

Cut the smaller piece of wadding to roughly the shape of the headboard and centre it on the stapled wadding. This piece helps to 'plump out' the upholstery.

Mark the middle of the headboard's top and bottom edges. Fold and then mark the middle of the fabric.

Spread the fabric over the headboard, matching the marks. Take the excess fabric over the edges and tack it temporarily (see Fig 2), pleating the fabric on the curved top edge for smoothness.

Buttoning Use the paper pattern to mark the position of the buttons. Punch a staple into the headboard through the fabric and wadding thicknesses to mark the button positions.

Sew the buttons to the headboard, using a curved needle (see Fig 3).

Staple the fabric to the back of the headboard, removing the temporary tacks as you work, keeping the curved edge smooth. Set the staples close to the edge. Trim the excess fabric away.

Glue the rope along the top edge and down both sides. Cut a few strands from the rope ends at the bottom corners of the headboard. Glue the ends under neatly. When the glue is dry, sew the rope to the headboard, working from the back (Fig 4).

Finishing

Cut the scrim to the shape of the headboard plus a 5cm (2in) allowance all round. Lay the bottom edge against the headboard, right side to the headboard. Set tacks along the bottom edge about 5cm (2in) apart. Pull the scrim up smoothly and temporarily tack along the curved top edge, turning the scrim edge under.

Turn the side edges under and set tacks in the middle of the sides, then tack towards the bottom corners and upwards to the top edge. Complete the tacking along the top edge.

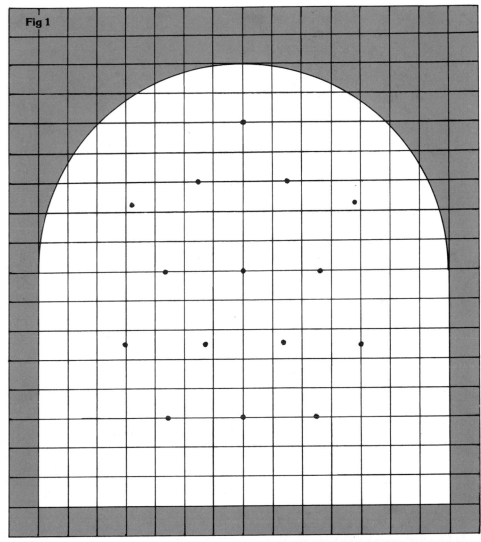

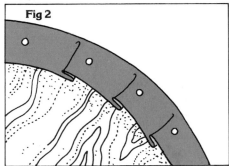

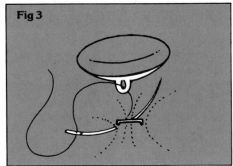

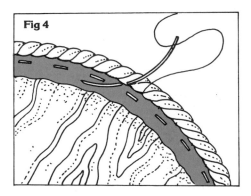

Fig 1 Graph pattern for the headboard: scale 1 sq = 10cm (4in). Mark in the button positions

Fig 2 Temporary-tack the fabric to the back of the headboard

Fig 3 Staple on the button position then sew on a button using a curved needle

Fig 4 Glue on the cord, then sew the cord to the fabric, using a curved needle, working from the back of the headboard

Frilled Austrian blind

Austrian blinds can be used in any room in the house but they look soft and pretty in a bedroom, particularly if the edge is frilled. Use either a semi-transparent fabric so that the light filters through or line the blind. The frilled blind in the picture has been lined.

Estimating materials

This type of blind is supported on cords threaded through screw eyes which have been inserted into the underside of a pelmet board. The blind in the picture also has a gathered heading which hooks onto a curtain track fixed to the front edge of the pelmet board.

The blind should hang in soft vertical folds like a curtain so the width of fabric should be 2–2½ times the width of the window frame. If widths of fabric need to be joined, do this with french seams (see page 64).

If the window is very wide, it is better to hang two or more Austrian blinds side by side rather than one wide blind.

To estimate the length of fabric required, measure from the curtain track to the window sill, plus 45cm (18in) for fullness plus a further 3cm (1¼in) for the top hem.

For the frill, measure round the sides and bottom edge of the blind and double the measurement. The frill piece will be 20cm (8in) wide. To estimate the length of piping cord required, measure the sides and bottom edge of the blind.

You will need about 1m (1⅛yd) of contrasting fabric for covering the piping, for a blind of average size.

Blind tapes can be anything from 30–60cm (12–24in) apart, depending on the effect required. The tapes on the blind pictured are about 30cm (12in) apart. Measure the proposed depth of the blind and add 5cm (2in) to each length of tape for top and bottom turnings.

Materials required

Blind fabric as estimated and the same amount of lining fabric
Pencil-pleat curtain heading tape to the width of the fabric plus turnings
Contrast fabric for piping
Piping cord
Austrian blind tape
Matching sewing threads
Strong nylon cord
Screw eyes
Wall hook fixing

Preparation

Cut bias strips from the contrasting fabric. Prepare the cord and cover with fabric (see page 10, Figs 2–6).

Join 20cm (8in)-wide strips of fabric to make the frill. Fold the strip down its length, wrong sides facing. Zigzag-stitch the raw edges together.

Join widths of fabric and lining, if necessary, using french seams.

Making the blind

Spread the blind fabric right side up. Gather and pin the frill round three sides, sandwiching the prepared piping between and matching raw edges. Baste and machine-stitch. Press the seam allowance upwards. Turn in and slipstitch the frill ends.

Turn 3cm (1¼in) to the wrong side on the top edge of the blind. Press and pin.

Spread the lining on the wrong side of the blind. Turn under a hem all round and slipstitch to the blind.

Still working on the wrong side of the blind, measure and mark the positions of the tapes.

Cut and pin the tapes to the blind, turning the ends under at the bottom edge but making sure that, as each piece of tape is cut, the loops align across the blind. Baste the tapes, then machine-stitch on both edges. Turn under the top edge neatly and stitch.

Pin and baste the curtain heading tape to the top edge of the blind. Machine-stitch and pull up the cords so that the blind is the same width as the curtain track. Insert the tape hooks.

Fixing the blind

Insert screw eyes into the underside of the pelmet board, setting them down the middle, and making sure that they correspond with the positions of the blind tapes.

Tie the cord end to the bottom loop on the tape which will lie furthest from the wall fixing (see Fig 1). Thread the cord through each loop in the tape, then through the screw eye above. Continue, threading the cord through each of the screw eyes and then cut the cord end, leaving enough to wind round the wall hook.

Thread each of the blind tapes in the same way, taking each cord end through the screw eye above the tape and then the adjacent screw eyes (see Fig 1). Gather the cord ends together and trim the ends to the same length. Plait the ends and knot them, to fasten round the wall hook.

Pull on the plaited cord end to gather up the blind as required.

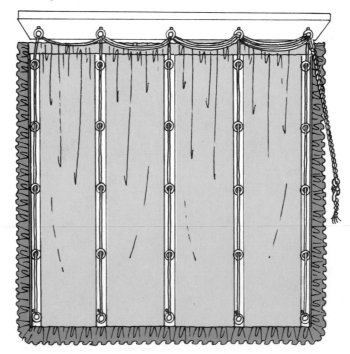

Fig 1 *The wrong side of the Austrian blind: The curtain track is fixed to the front edge of the pelmet board. Ring hooks are screwed into the underside of the board to carry the blind's cords*

Bedroom gifts

Pretty accessories for the bedroom can be made very simply and are an ideal way of using odd pieces of fabrics left over from other sewing projects.

All the accessories in the picture would make perfect gifts – if you can bear to part with them.

Dress hanger

Fabric-covered hangers are essential for soft clothing, such as dresses–blouses and the method for making them given here is both simple and quick.

Materials required

For one wooden hanger
50 × 10cm *(20 × 4in)* of 1cm *(³⁄₈in)*-
   thick polyester wadding
70 × 14cm *(28 × 5¹⁄₂in)* piece of
   lightweight fabric
50 × 3cm *(20 × 1¹⁄₄in)* bias-cut strip of
   the same fabric
All-purpose adhesive
Matching sewing thread

Preparation

Check the coat hanger for any roughness and smooth the surface and edges with fine sandpaper.

Fold one long edge of the bias-cut strip 1cm *(³⁄₈in)* to the wrong side and press.

Making the hanger

Spread a little adhesive over the hook of the hanger. Fold the bias-cut strip over the hook, with the folded edge uppermost, and bind the fabric round the hook very tightly. Twist the end round the hanger itself and secure with a few stitches. Cut a small hole in the centre of the piece of wadding and slip it over the hook. Bring the long edges together under the hanger and oversew them.

Covering the hanger Place the hanger on the wrong side of the fabric and bring the long edges together along the top edge. Turn a 1cm *(³⁄₈in)* hem to the wrong side on both edges and pin them together.

Thread a needle with a long length of thread. Starting at the hook, sew the edges together using small running stitches. Work from the hook, round the end of the hanger and to the middle of the underside (Fig 1). Draw up the gathers and secure the thread end with a double backstitch.

Gather the other side of the hanger in the same way.

Decorating hangers

A covered dress hanger can be decorated with a ribbon bow, tied round the hook.

For a special gift, make a lavender-filled sachet from a 15cm *(6in)* piece of 7.5cm *(3in)*-wide satin ribbon, or from a small scrap of fabric or lace. Tie the sachet to the hook.

Silk flowers, or flowers made of ribbons or lace also look pretty tied to the hanger.

Slippers

Fabric slippers are perfect for wearing in the bedroom and have the advantage of being soft and light enough to pack for travelling. A draw string storage bag could be made in the same fabric.

Materials required

For 2 slippers of either size
60 × 38cm *(24 × 15in)* piece of fabric
   38cm *(15in)* square of thick woollen
   fabric
38cm *(15in)* square of firm card
60 × 38cm *(24 × 15in)* piece of soft
   cotton curtain interlining (or
   polyester wadding)
1.60m *(1³⁄₄yd)* of 2cm *(³⁄₄in)*-wide flat
   woven braid

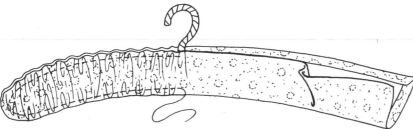

Fig 1 *Starting at the hook, work running stitches through both thicknesses of fabric, pulling up gathers as you work. Sew to the middle of the underside, then work along the other side of the hanger in exactly the same way*

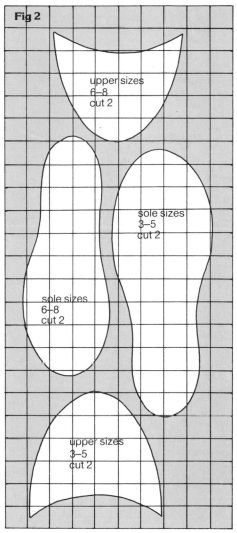

Fig 2 *Graph pattern for the soft slippers: scale 1 sq = 2.5cm (1in)*

Preparation

Fig 2 is the graph pattern for the slippers and two sizes are given, sizes 3–5 and 6–8. (US sizes 4½–6½ and 7½–9½, and European sizes 35–38 and 39–41). The scale is 1 square = 2.5cm (1in). Draw the selected pattern pieces to scale on squared pattern paper. The patterns include a 6mm (¼in) seam allowance all round.

Cut out the patterns. Using the sole pattern cut two shapes from the fabric, the interlining or wadding, the card and from the thick woollen fabric.

Using the upper pattern, cut four pieces from the fabric and two from the interlining or wadding.

Making a slipper

Lay the woollen fabric right side down and then place on top the card, then the interlining or wadding and finally the

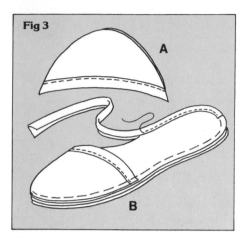

Fig 3 *Stitch the three layers of the uppers together, then bind the front edge with braid (A). Machine-stitch the four layers of the sole together, stitch on the uppers and bind with braid all round (B)*

fabric, right side up. Match all the edges. Pin together all round and then baste. Set the sewing machine to a long stitch and stitch 6mm (*1/4in*) from the edge all round, working through all the thicknesses.

Uppers

Place the interlining on the wrong side of one fabric piece, then put the second fabric piece on top, right side up. Pin and baste together, matching the edges. Machine-stitch all round through all thicknesses.

Finishing

Cut a piece of braid to fit along the front edge of the upper piece. Fold the braid over the raw edges and pin. Baste and then machine-stitch the braid to the upper through all thicknesses (Fig 3a).

Pin and then baste the upper to the sole, fitting the edges of the upper to

the edges of the sole. Fold and pin the braid round the welt of the slipper, starting at the middle of the back edge (see Fig 3b). Baste the braid round the slipper, folding the raw ends under and butting them together neatly.

Machine-stitch the braid to the slipper, working through all the thicknesses. Make a second slipper in the same way.

Note: if you experience difficulty in machine-stitching the upper to the sole, this stage can be worked with hand-sewing, using backstitch.

Nightdress case

This is simply made by folding and stitching interlined fabric into an envelope. Cases such as this can also be made for handkerchiefs or scarves.

Materials required

Finished size 28 × 38cm (*11 × 15in*)
80cm (*32in*) square of fine cotton lawn
80 × 40cm (*32 × 16in*) piece of soft cotton interlining (or wadding)
2m (*2¹/4yd*) of 15mm (*5/8in*)-wide cotton bias binding
Press fastener
Matching sewing thread

Preparation

Following Fig 4, draw a paper pattern to the dimensions given. Cut the fabric in half. Use the pattern to cut both pieces of fabric and the interlining.

Making the case

Lay one piece of the fabric wrong side up and lay the interlining on top. Lay the second piece of fabric on top.

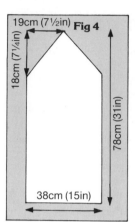

Fig 4 *Copy the measurements on this chart to make a pattern for the nightdress or pyjama case*

Fig 5 *Bind the case pocket with binding, then bind all round the edges*

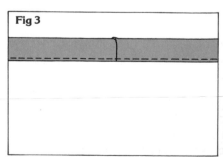

Pin and baste the layers together on the edges. Machine-stitch on all edges, taking a 6mm (*1/4in*) seam allowance. Trim the seam allowance back to 3mm (*1/8in*). Apply the bias binding to the short, bottom edge (see Figs 1, 2, 3).

Fold up the edge to make a 28cm (*11in*)-deep pocket. Pin the sides together. Baste close to the edges. Apply bias binding on both side edges and round the pointed flap (Fig 5).

Finishing

Cut a piece of bias binding 45cm (*18in*) long and fold it along the length. Machine-stitch and neaten the ends with sewing. Tie a bow, leaving long ends, and sew to the case flap. Sew a press fastener under the flap to secure the case.

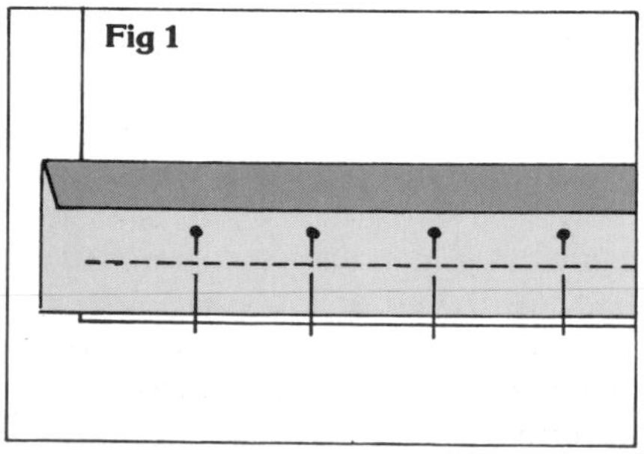

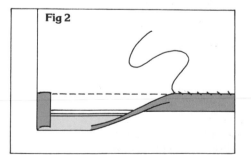

Applying bias binding
Fig 1 *Pin then baste the binding to the fabric matching edges. Machine-stitch*

Fig 2 *Turn the binding to the wrong side and hem or slip-stitch*

Fig 3 *To join the ends of bias binding, turn the cut ends to the wrong side about 3mm (1/8in), overlap one over the other and secure with stitching*

Pleated lampshade

The lampshade in the picture on page 37 is very easy to make and the technique can be adapted to both conical and drum-shaped shades. Single rings can also be used to make the shade.

Estimating materials

Measure the frame from the top ring to the bottom ring and add 5cm (2in). Measure the circumference of the larger ring and double the measurement. Add 2.5cm (1in). This gives you the dimensions of paper and fabric required for the lampshade. Measure the circumference of both rings for the quantity of bias binding and ribbon, adding 20cm (8in) to the ribbon quantity for a bow.

Materials required

Plastic-coated or white-painted
   lampshade frame (or two separate
   rings)
Fabric as estimated
Stiff paper to the same size as fabric
Bias binding
6mm (1/4in)-wide ribbon
White button thread
Clear adhesive fabric

Tools required

Hole punch

Preparation

Spread adhesive thinly on the paper. Smooth the fabric onto the paper and leave to dry.

Using a sharply pointed pencil, measure and mark points 2cm (3/4in) apart along the top and bottom edges and on both sides of the fabric-covered paper. Glue bias binding along the top and bottom edges of the shade. Leave to dry.

Making the shade

Using a metal rule and a blunt-tipped needle, score between the pleat marks on the paper side of the shade. This will help you to make sharp-edged folds (Fig 6a). Fold concertina pleats, drawing the edge of the metal rule across each fold as it is made, to sharpen it. Measure and mark the centre of each pleat 2cm (3/4in) down from the top edge for eyelet holes.

Punch holes through the marks as shown in Fig 6b.

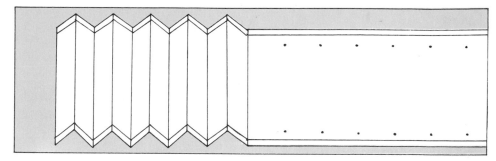

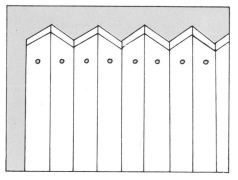

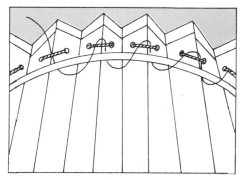

Fig 6a *Cover the fabric edges with binding; mark points 18mm (3/4in) apart on top and bottom edges, fold and crease the pleats*

Fig 6b *Punch holes through the pleats*

Fig 6c *Thread narrow ribbon through the punched holes, then sew the shade to the frame, taking stitches over the bound ring and under the ribbon*

Finishing

Overlap the pleats at the ends and glue the overlap, to form the shade. The join should be in the middle of a pleat.

Thread ribbon through the holes and tie the ends in a bow, so that the shade fits the top ring of the frame.

Slip the shade onto the frame and secure the shade to the frame by working stitches through the ribbon loops and round the ring (see Fig 6c.)

If two separate rings are being used, punch holes at both top and bottom edges of the pleated shade and thread ribbon through, joining the ends with a few stitches on the inside of the shade. Work stitches through the ribbon loops and round the ring in the way described.

Quilted case

This design has a dual use: some people, who still prefer a rubber hot water bottle to an electric blanket, will want it as a neat cover for the bottle.

The design also makes a plain and simple case for pyjamas.

Materials required

Finished size 38 × 30cm (15 × 12in)
63 × 42cm (25 × 16 1/2in) of quilted, washable two-sided fabric

2m (2 1/4yd) of 15mm (5/8in)-wide bias binding
2 self-stick fastener discs or 2 press fasteners
Matching sewing thread

Preparation

Cut the fabric in two pieces, each 42 × 31cm (16 1/2 × 12 1/2in). Pin the pieces together and mark round all the corners using a small plate or a saucer as a guide. Cut the four corners through both thicknesses.

Making the case

Bind the curved top edge on both pieces. The binding should not go beyond the end of the curves – about 10cm (4in) down the sides.

With back and front pieces wrong sides facing, pin and baste the side and bottom edges together. Machine-stitch 6mm (1/4in) from the edge. Trim the seam allowance back to 3mm (1/8in) and bind with bias binding.

Sew the self-stick fasteners to the inside top edges, or apply press fasteners.

If desired, stitch the remaining short length of bias binding along its length and sew it into a decorative bow, as shown on the Nightdress case (see the picture on page 37).

Kitchens

Sewing for your kitchen is rewarding because, with the vast range of fabrics available, co-ordinated effects are easy to achieve. The bright yellow and pale grey scheme for the kitchen accessories pictured is just one option – choose colours and patterns to suit your own ideas.

Sunshine kitchen set

Tablecloth

PVC-coated fabric is a good choice for a kitchen tablecloth, particularly when young children are around. Food spills can be quickly cleaned away with a damp cloth. This type of fabric does not fray and there is no necessity to hem the edges. If pieces require to be joined, hold seam edges together with paper clips or with pieces of self-adhesive tape. Do not use pins or basting, and do not iron or press PVC-coated fabrics. Machine-stitch using a long stitch (Fig 1).

Refer to page 4 for estimating fabrics for tablecloths.

Materials required
PVC-coated fabric
Matching polyester sewing thread

Making the tablecloth
If the hem is to be stitched, turn a 15mm *(⅝in)* hem and crease it with the back of a knife blade. Machine-stitch with a long stitch, 9mm *(⅜in)*

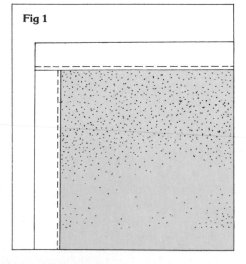

Fig 1

from the folded edge, turning the corners under neatly (Fig 1).

Pot warmer

It is surprising how an old-fashioned kitchen accessory such as a pot warmer can look acceptable in a modern kitchen if the fabric is carefully chosen.

The shape of the pot warmer pictured is designed so that it can be used for a coffee or tea pot – or even for a casserole dish.

Materials required
Finished size 27 × 35cm (10¾ × 14in)
54 × 35cm *(21 × 14in)* piece of cotton fabric
The same amount in lining fabric and polyester wadding
1.60m *(1¾yd)* of 15mm *(⅝in)*-wide bias binding
Matching sewing thread

Preparation
Cut the fabric, the lining and the polyester wadding into two pieces, each measuring 27 × 35cm *(10¾ × 14in)*. Lay one lining piece wrong side up, lay the wadding on top and then the fabric, right side up, matching the edges. Arrange the remaining fabric, wadding and lining in the same way. These are the back and front pieces of the pot warmer.

Pin the three layers of the back piece together and cut rounded corners on the top edge, following the technique shown on page 43, Fig 2. Work the front of the pot warmer in the same way.

Making the pot warmer
Baste the edges of the back piece together and work one or two rows of basting across the width also, to prepare the fabrics for quilting. Work the front piece in the same way.

Fig 1 *If the cloth needs a hem, crease with a knife blade then machine-stitch*

2 Window dressings

Kitchen windows can look just as decorative as any other window in the home and, if the family eat in the kitchen, pretty curtains are doubly important, especially in winter. Fabrics must be practical and easily laundered and thus cotton or sheer polyester fabrics are most suitable.

The techniques described for making unlined curtains (page 15) can be used for making kitchen curtains, both full and half length. Half-length curtains, called café curtains, are useful if the window is overlooked and yet maximum daylight is desired.

Blinds

Roller blinds and Roman blinds are both suitable for kitchen windows. Where modern kitchen units tend to make the room look functional, a pretty blind will soften the effect. Instructions for making roller blinds are on pages 44–45.

Fig 1 *Sew curtain rings to the top edge of unlined curtains. Hang the curtains on a brass or wooden pole.*

Fig 2 *Scalloped café curtains are made by cutting scallops in the doubled curtain heading, using a saucer as a guide. Machine-stitch the curve, then cut the scallops away (Fig 2a). Curtain rings are sewn to the tabs between scallops on the right side. Scalloped headings can also be made by cutting scallops in single thickness fabric, finishing the raw edges on the wrong side with bias binding*

Fig 3 *Sew pinch pleat heading along the top edge of sheer curtains. Insert curtain hooks which then fit into curtain rings*

Fig 4 *An alternative café curtain effect is achieved by sewing neatened 20cm (8in) tabs along the top edge of a curtain. Slip a curtain pole through the tabs*

Fig 5 *Use a painted or wood-stained dowel rod to hang lightweight curtains. Make a casing with a frill along the top edge (see page 14 Fig 3), then push the dowel through the casing, supporting the ends on large cup hooks*

Fig 1

Fig 3

Quilting

The pot warmer in the picture is made from a checked fabric and the lines of the check have been used as a guide for working machine-stitched quilting.

If the fabric you are using is a plain colour or has an all-over pattern, mark quilting lines 5cm *(2in)* apart, starting with a line down the middle, using a chalk pencil.

Set the sewing machine to a medium-length stitch and work along the marked lines. (If preferred, quilting can be worked by hand using Running stitches). Begin stitching on the middle line.

Quilt the front and back pieces in the same way.

When the quilting has been completed, bind the bottom, long edge on both the back and the front piece with bias binding, using the technique shown on page 38, Figs 1, 2, 3.

Finishing

Pin the front and back pieces together, matching edges, and baste.

Machine-stitch round the pot warmer, taking a 6mm *(¼in)* seam. Trim the seam allowance back to 3mm *(⅛in)*.

Bind the sides and top, curved edge of the pot warmer, using the same technique as that used for the bottom edges.

Fold and machine-stitch a 15cm *(6in)* strip of bias binding along its length. Fold the ends under and form the strip into a loop. Sew or machine-stitch the loop to the top of the pot warmer.

Tray mat

The quilted tray mat can be used as a breakfast tray, or for a TV dinner.

The quilting technique used is the same as that used for making the pot warmer.

Preparation

Measure the tray to obtain the dimensions of fabric, wadding and lining required. Measure round the tray to estimate the amount of bias binding required. If the tray is round or oval make a newspaper pattern.

Cut the fabric, wadding and lining to size and shape. Pin and baste the three fabrics together, as described for making the pot warmer.

Making the tray mat

The tray mat pictured has been quilted in 5cm *(2in)* squares, following the lines of the checked fabric. If the fabric being used is plain-coloured or has an all-over pattern, measure and draw the quilting lines using a chalk pencil. Measure and mark the vertical and horizontal middle lines first.

Round off all four corners using a cup or glass as a guide (Fig 2).

Set the sewing machine to a medium-length stitch and machine-stitch the horizontal lines first, beginning with the middle line, then stitch the vertical lines, again beginning with the middle line.

Finishing

Machine-stitch the three layers together on the edges, taking a 6mm *(¼in)* seam. Trim the seam allowance back to 3mm *(⅛in)* and bind the edges with bias binding using the technique described on page 38.

Join the ends by turning the edges under, then overlapping one end on the other. Complete the machine-stitching. Make matching table napkins by cutting 40cm *(16in)* squares of cotton fabric and applying bias binding to the edges.

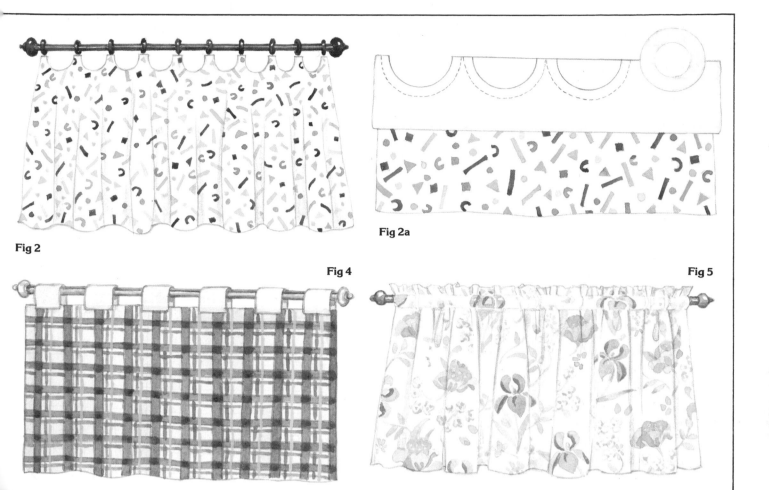

Fig 2

Fig 2a

Fig 4

Fig 5

Pot holder

Padded pot holders are an essential item in the kitchen. Made in an stylish fabric and trimmed with a brightly coloured bias binding, they also make an attractive accessory.

Materials required

Finished size 70 × 20cm (28 × 8in)
110 × 20cm (43 × 8in) piece of cotton fabric
The same amount in a constrasting fabric for lining and in polyester wadding
2.30m (2½yd) of 15mm (⅝in)-wide cotton bias binding
Matching sewing thread

Preparation

Mark the fabric with vertical and horizontal lines 5cm (2in) apart to make a squared quilting pattern.

Making the pot holder

Lay the wadding on the wrong side of the lining fabric and lay the marked fabric on top, right side up.

Baste together round the edges and across the width about one-third and two-thirds down from the top edge.

Machine-stitch along the marked lines, starting with the middle vertical and horizontal lines.

When the quilting is completed, remove the basting threads and then bind the short ends with bias binding.

Fold the two short ends towards the middle making pockets 20cm (8in) deep. Pin along the sides.

Using a saucer or a small plate, mark and cut rounded corners (Fig 2).

Bind all round the pot holder, following the same technique used for the pocket edges.

Cut a strip of binding 15cm (6in) long. Fold along the length and machine-stitch. Turn under the ends and form the strip into a loop. Sew or stitch the loop to the middle of one long edge of the pot holder (see picture).

Fig 2 *Fold in the ends of the quilted piece 20cm (8in) and pin. Use a small plate to mark the curved ends of the holder*

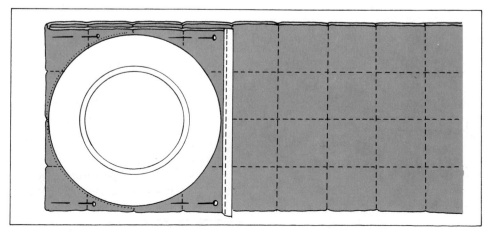

Roller blind

This kind of blind is very often the best choice for a kitchen window, as an area of plain colour and simple lines looks good with most styles of kitchen units. The blind pictured is made with a fabric that has been stiffened with a special fabric spray but pre-stiffened blind fabrics are available in furnishing fabric shops and department stores.

Estimating materials

Depending on the style of the window, the blind will either be positioned inside the window recess or above and outside the window frame (see Figs 1a and 1b).

In a recess, the blind brackets are fitted to the sides of the window frame. Measure the width of the roller for the fabric width – no turnings are necessary on the side edges. Measure from the roller to the bottom of the frame or the window sill and add 30cm (12in) so that there is sufficient fabric to cover the roller and for the batten tuck.

If the blind is to be fixed above the window frame, it should be long enough to extend at least 4cm (1½in) each side of the window frame and be positioned 5cm (2in) above the window (Fig 1b).

Estimate the width of fabric by measuring the roller and estimate the fabric length in the same way as for the recessed blind. For both types of window, add an extra 14cm (5½in) to the length of fabric for hem backing.

Although the method described here can be adapted to blinds of any width, blinds are best confined to fairly narrow windows so that it is not necessary to join widths of fabric. Joins tend to prevent the smooth running of the blind onto the roller.

Materials required

Roller blind, complete with fixtures
Pre-stiffened blind fabric as estimated
Fabric stiffener if ordinary fabric is
    being used
Flat wooden batten to the blind width
Paper for pattern
Fabric adhesive
Curtain ring and crochet cotton
    (optional)

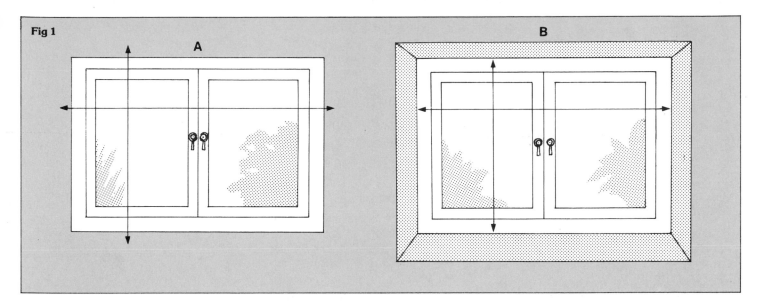

Preparation

If the fabric is to be stiffened, hang it outdoors and spray on both sides, following the manufacturer's instructions. Leave to dry.

Both pre-stiffened fabrics and spray-stiffened fabrics must be cut absolutely square on the ends so that the fabric winds straight onto the roller.

Spread the fabric flat and measure and mark straight ends using a ruler or T-square. Cut the fabric with a crafts knife and ruler or with a pair of sharp scissors.

Following Fig 2, cut a paper pattern for the blind edging. The blind pictured has points 13cm *(5¹/₈in)* deep and 18cm *(7¹/₈in)* across the widest point. Half-points should fall at the edges of the blind and it may be necessary to adjust the dimensions of the points to suit your width of fabric.

Lay the pattern on the end of the blind fabric and cut out for backing the blind hem.

Making the blind

Using the paper pattern, cut the bottom edge of the fabric in points to match the prepared backing. Glue the backing piece to the wrong side of the blind, taking care to match the points. Trim edges of the points edges if necessary for a neat finish.

Fold and stitch a casing for the batten along the bottom of the blind, just above the points (see Fig 3).

Stitch across the blind just below the casing and then round the points and along the sides of the blind to the depth of the points (Fig 3).

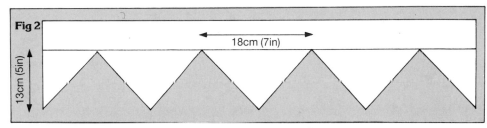

Slip the batten into the casing.

Screw the cord holder (supplied with the blind kit) into the middle of the batten. If a pull has not been supplied, make a ring toggle by working Buttonhole stitch over a curtain ring, using crochet cotton, and fasten this to the cord.

Finishing

Fix the top edge of the blind to the roller using adhesive and tacks, following the manufacturer's instructions and taking care to see that the edge of the blind is straight along the roller. Fix the roller into the brackets.

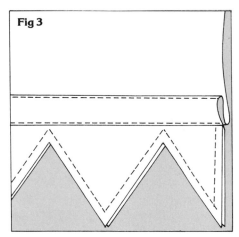

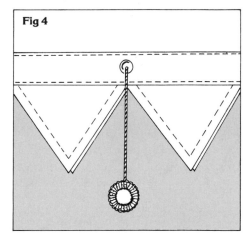

Fig 1 *Measure flush windows from 3cm (1¹/₈in) below and each side of the window frame, and from 5cm (2in) above the frame (A). Measure for recessed windows by measuring the depth and width of the frame (B)*

Fig 2 *Diagram for the pointed edge. Half of a point should be allowed at the ends. Adjust the width or the points to fit your blind*

Fig 3 *Make and stitch a tuck in the blind for the batten, 12.5cm (5in) from the bottom edge. Stitch across under the batten tuck, then cut the points*

Fig 4 *Make a blind pull from a plastic curtain ring, covered with Buttonhole stitch. Pierce a hole in the batten and glue the cord end in the hole on the wrong side*

Bathrooms

The bathroom may not, at first, seem an obvious place for sewing projects but with the move towards making the bathroom a place to linger in, luxurious accessories become important furnishings. Satin-trimmed towels and a soft bathmat are two ideas for you to try.

Towel trims

Whether towels are made from lengths of towelling or are purchased ready-made, pretty trims can be added to bring colour and a touch of luxury into the bathroom. The ideas here can also be used to make charming wedding or anniversary gifts.

Towel set

Finished sizes: bath towel 130 × 90cm (52 × 36in), 2 small towels 70 × 90cm (28 × 36in)

Materials required

2.75m *(3yd)* of 90cm *(36in)*-wide
   towelling
Edgings and trims as desired
Matching sewing threads

Preparation

Wash towelling before cutting to enable any shrinkage to take place. Trim off the selvedges. Cut the towelling into pieces as follows: bath towel, 130 × 90cm *(52 × 36in)*, two smaller towels, 70 × 90cm *(28 × 36in)*.

Work zigzag machine-stitching on all the cut edges immediately to prevent the towelling from fraying.

Satin bias binding

Measure round the towel, adding 2.5cm *(1in)* to the measurement for the amount of satin bias binding required.

Beginning in the middle of one side, apply the binding to the towel edges.

Bias-cut strips of patterned or plain cotton fabric can be used instead of prepared bias binding.

Broderie anglaise and ribbon

Bind the edges of the towel with cotton bias binding. Work zigzag machine-stitching along the binding edges for additional strength and a pretty finish.

Pin and baste broderie anglaise insert across the towel, tucking the ends under at the edges. Machine-stitch the broderie along both edges and across the ends, then thread washable polyester satin ribbon through the slots (Fig 1). Finish the ribbon ends with hand-sewing.

Lace edging

Cotton lace edging can be applied so that the lace hangs below the towel edge or it can be stitched to the towel

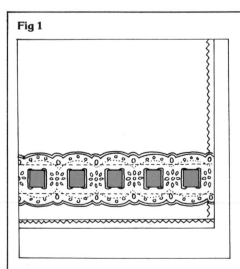

Fig 1 *Stitch ribbon-threaded broderie anglaise along the towel hems*

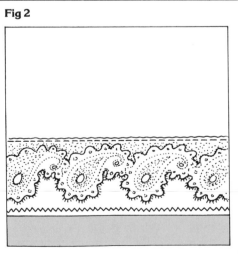

Fig 2 *Stitch deep cotton lace about 2.5cm (1in) from the edge*

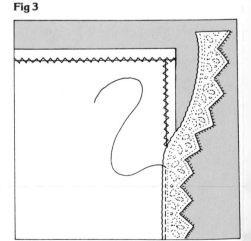

Fig 3 *Neaten the edges with zigzag stitching then apply lace edging over the neatened edge*

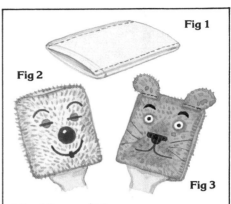

Bath mitts

If a number of towels are being made there may be pieces of towelling left over.

Bath mitts are quick and simple to make and they are particularly popular with children.

Cut 45 × 18cm *(18 × 7¼in)* strips. Turn and machine-stitch a narrow hem on both short ends. Fold across the width, right sides facing and machine-stitch the sides to make a mitt (Fig 1). Faces can be embroidered on mitts, using washable and colourfast embroidery threads (Fig 2). By adding ears, animal mitts can be made to amuse very small children at bathtime (Fig 3).

along the straight edge only, using straight stitch or zigzag stitch (Figs 2 and 3).

Appliqué ribbon

Washable polyester satin or grosgrain ribbons are available in both plain colours and patterns and make good trims for bathroom towels. To apply ribbon, turn the edges of the towel to the right side and then baste the ribbon over the turning, aligning the ribbon edge with the folded edge. Machine-stitch along both edges, folding the ribbon into a mitre at corners as shown in (Fig 4).

Motifs and initials

Motifs and initials cut from washable fabrics are an ideal way of personalising towels. Cut out the motifs and apply to towels, following the technique described on page 11. The shell motif pattern Fig 1 on page 11 would look pretty applied to a set of towels.

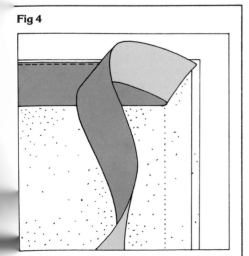

Fig 4 *Machine-stitch ribbon on the outer edge, fold a mitre, continue stitching. Then stitch the inner edge*

Ocean wave bathmat

The bathmat is made of softly-padded absorbent towelling but it can be left on the bathroom floor as a washable rug. Shades of blue and grey have been used to simulate the colours of the sea.

Materials required

Finished size 91 × 58cm (36 × 23in)
91 × 58cm *(36 × 23in)* plain towelling for backing
91 × 58cm *(36 × 23in)* of 3cm *(1¼in)*-thick polyester wadding
20 × 91cm *(8 × 36in)* pieces of towelling in 5 different colours, white, grey, light blue, medium blue and dark blue
3.65m *(4yd)* of narrow washable cotton braid
Matching sewing threads

Preparation

From Fig 1, draw the pattern pieces for the waves to full size on squared pattern paper (scale 1 sq = 10cm *(4in)*.

Pin each pattern piece to coloured towelling and cut out the waves.

Making the bathmat

Spread the backing towelling and lay the wadding on top. Baste all round the edges and across the wadding, approximately one-third and two-thirds down from the top edge. Trim any excess wadding from the edges.

Lay the white wave first, matching the top edges with the backing fabric. Pin and then arrange the grey wave so that it just overlaps the white wave. Pin, baste and then machine-stitch along the wavy edge, using a wide zigzag stitch (Fig 2). Arrange the subsequent waves in the same way, following the arrangement of colours indicated in the pattern (Fig 1).

Measure the mat to see that the corners are square.

Lay the narrow braid along the zigzag-stitched lines between the waves and, using a straight stitch, machine-stitch along the middle of the braid. Trim the braid ends level with the mat edges.

Finishing

Baste the edges of the mat. Work a closely-spaced, wide zigzag stitch over the edges. If preferred, the edges can be finished with bias binding or bias-cut strips of washable cotton fabric.

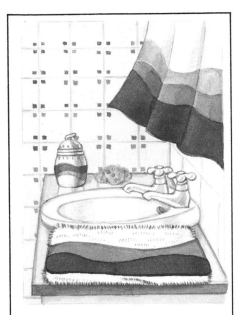

Sea theme

A simple design theme, such as the ocean wave pattern can be used to good effect in a bathroom. White cotton curtains can be edged with waves. Reduce the depth of each wave to about half and apply them in the same way as described for the bathmat but begin with the dark blue at the hem, and tuck each subsequent wave under the curved edge as it is stitched.

The theme could also be extended by applying one or two waves to the edges of bathroom towels.

Pick up the colours of the waves – the bath mat pictured uses a blue scheme but this can be adapted to your own decor – in small ceramic jars and pots.

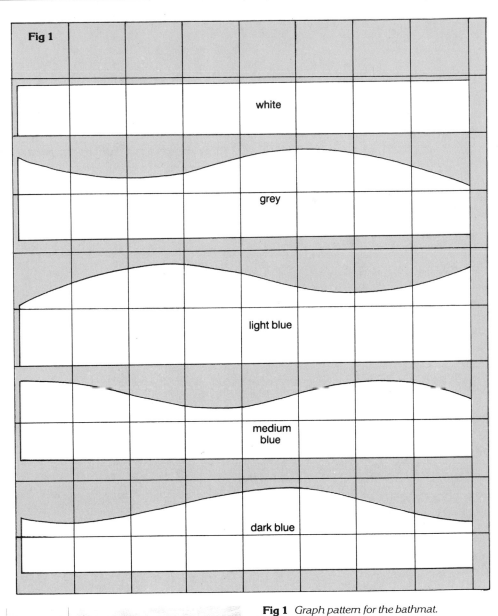

white

grey

light blue

medium blue

dark blue

Fig 1 *Graph pattern for the bathmat.*

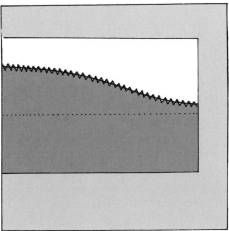

Fig 2 *Overlap the first, grey wave on the white strip and zigzag-stitch along the edge.*

Young Ideas

Sewing for babies and children is satisfying and rewarding because you can create something original that cannot readily be found in the shops. A lined baby basket and quilt, and perhaps, a set of crib bumpers, might be your first projects to welcome a new baby.

Lined baby basket

Lined wicker baskets make delightful beds for new babies – the lining keeps the basket clean and free from draughts. Make a crisp broderie anglaise quilt, edged with a double fabric frill to go with the basket.

Baby basket

For a basket with a 75 × 28cm (30 × 11in) base

Materials required
Patterned cotton fabric
6mm (¼in)-wide elastic
15mm (⅝) bias binding
Matching sewing thread
For the quilt
Broderie anglaise
White cotton fabric
Polyester wadding

Estimating fabric
Most baby baskets are of the same size but it is advisable to measure the basket before buying fabric.

Measure the length and width of the basket bottom. Add 2.5cm (1in) to both measurements.

Measure round the top edge of the basket and add half the measurement. Measure the depth of the basket at the head end and add 10cm (4in). These measurements give you the quantity of fabric required.

Preparation
Lay the basket on a large sheet of paper and draw round it to make a pattern for the basket bottom.

Use this pattern to cut out the base piece, adding 12mm (½in) seam allowance all round.

Making the lining
Cut the main lining piece to the maximum depth of the basket plus 10cm (4in), by the circumference of the top edge plus half of the measurement.

Join the short ends of the main lining piece with a french seam (see page 64).

Gather the bottom edge with two rows of gathering stitches. Draw up the threads so that the lining fits the bottom piece. Pin the lining to the bottom piece, right sides of fabric facing.

Baste and then machine-stitch, taking a 12mm (½in) seam.

Finish the seam edges with zigzag machine-stitching.

Put the lining into the basket and roughly pin it through the wicker.

Cut the top edge to follow the shape of the basket but still leaving a 10cm (4in) allowance all round (see Fig 1).

Bind the top edge with bias binding to make a casing, leaving a gap in the binding seam for inserting the elastic.

Cut a piece of elastic to fit round the basket just under the rim plus 2.5cm (1in). Thread the elastic through the casing and sew the elastic ends together. Close the binding seam.

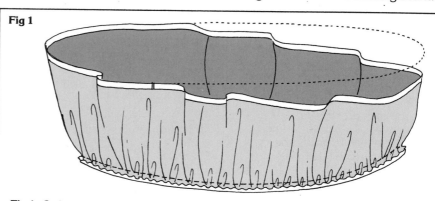

Fig 1 *Gather the lining and then machine-stitch to the base, right sides facing. Trim the top edge to the basket shape, leaving a 10cm (4in) allowance. Bind the edge for a casing*

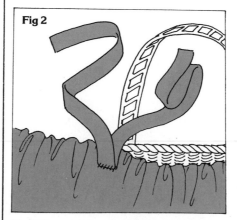

Fig 2 *Sew the tie strips to the inside of the lining, level with the handles*

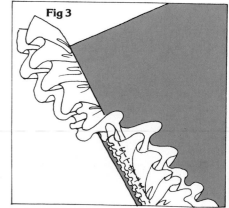

Fig 3 *Run gathering stitches through both frills and apply them to the quilt as one*

Fit the lining into the basket. Mark where the side handles fall with pins.

Making ties

Cut four 56 × 9cm *(22 × 3½in)*-wide strips of fabric. Fold each strip lengthways, right sides facing. Machine-stitch the edges together to make ties (refer to page 53, Fig 4).

Sew each tie to the lining where it meets the basket handles (Fig 2). Knot the ties round the handles.

Baby quilt

The quilt is made from white broderie anglaise, backed with plain white cotton fabric. It is edged with a double frill, one in white cotton fabric and the other in the patterned fabric used for lining the basket.

Preparation

Use the basket base pattern to cut the quilt fabrics. Trim 20cm *(8in)* from the head end of the pattern.

Cut the shape from broderie anglaise, polyester wadding and from white cotton fabric, adding 15mm *(⅝in)* all round on all pieces.

Measure the sides of the pattern and across the bottom end, adding half the total measurement for the length of the frills. Cut the white frill strip 8cm *(3¼in)* wide and the patterned frill 6cm *(2½in)* wide.

Making the quilt

Make the frills first. Fold each strip lengthways and gather the raw edges together. Pull up the threads to fit the sides and bottom edge of the quilt. Tuck in the ends, press and then close with slip stitches.

Lay the broderie anglaise on the wadding and baste together round the edges. Arrange the frill round the quilt, matching the edges. The white frill lies on the broderie anglaise with the patterned frill on top. Baste and machine-stitch the frills to the quilt. Press the frills away from the quilt (Fig 3).

Lay the backing on top, right sides facing.

Baste and machine-stitch across the top edge (taking care not to catch in the ends of the frills).

Turn the backing to the wadding side of the quilt. Turn in the edges all round and slipstitch to the quilt.

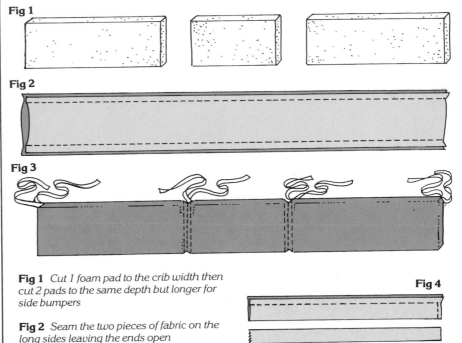

Fig 1

Fig 2

Fig 3

Fig 1 *Cut 1 foam pad to the crib width then cut 2 pads to the same depth but longer for side bumpers*

Fig 2 *Seam the two pieces of fabric on the long sides leaving the ends open*

Fig 3 *Push the foam pads in through the ends with 37mm (1½in) between. Slipstitch ends, machine-stitch hinges*

Fig 4

Fig 4 *Making ties: fold the fabric right sides facing and machine-stitch. Turn right sides out.*

Crib bumpers

This is an excellent idea for keeping cold draughts from the crib and for protecting the baby's head from the bars. Bumpers have a soft foam padding and both this and the outer fabric should be flame-retardant. Tie the bumpers to the crib so that they can be removed easily.

Estimating materials

Measure the inside width of the crib. You will need a piece of 2.5cm *(1in)*-thick foam to this measurement by 20cm *(8in)*. The side bumpers each measure 60cm *(24in)* long by 20cm *(8in)* deep and you will need two pieces of 2.5cm *(1in)*-thick foam to these measurements.

To estimate the width of fabric required, lay the three foam bumpers side by side as shown in Fig 1, with 4cm *(1½in)* between them.

Measure the overall length and add 5cm *(2in)*. The width of fabric required is 20cm *(8in)* plus 5cm *(2in)*.

Materials required

2 pieces of fabric to the estimated length and width
4 strips 45 × 4cm *(18 × 1½in)* for ties
2 pieces of 2.5cm *(1in)*-thick foam for side bumpers, 1 piece of foam for the headboard bumper
Matching sewing threads

Preparation

Make the ties by folding each strip lengthways, right sides facing.

Machine-stitch the long edges, turn to the right side and turn in the open ends. Slipstitch to close (Fig 4).

Making the bumpers

Pin and baste together the long edges of the fabric pieces, then machine-stitch taking a 12mm *(½in)* seam (Fig 2). Turn the casing to the right side. Push the headboard bumper into the casing, positioning it in the middle. Push the side bumpers in from each end, leaving approximately 4cm *(1½in)* between the bumpers. Pin and baste between the foam bumpers to make hinges. Turn in the casing ends and slipstitch or machine-stitch to close.

Make the hinges between the bumpers by machine-stitching along the basted lines, working rows of stitches 6mm *(¼in)* apart (Fig 3).

Fold the ties and stitch to the top edge of the bumper as shown in Fig 3.

Soft play ring

This looks like a large project but in fact only simple sewing is involved, although quite large quantities of fabric are needed.

The play ring will amuse a child from the baby stage through to eight or nine years old, when the ring becomes part of imaginative games or a private place to curl up in. Two different fabrics have been used to make the play ring but fabric scraps could be used, if preferred.

Materials required
1.80m *(2yd)* each of two different
    cotton fabrics
90cm *(36in)* square of cotton fabric
Large bag of flame-retardant filling
24 buttons 2.5cm *(1in)*-diameter
2m *(2¼yd)* of 6mm *(¼in)*-wide ribbon
Matching sewing thread

Preparation
Cut the two fabrics into 18cm *(7in)*-wide strips and join them on the short ends to make 3.50m *(3¾yd)* lengths. Make 8 long strips in this way.

Making the ring
Machine-stitch the strips together on the long sides. Fold the piece in half right sides facing (Fig 1). Machine-stitch the edges together. Baste along the seams through both thicknesses of fabric. Machine-stitch along the seams to make four divisions.

Fold in the raw ends on one end and machine-stitch to close.

Using a long stick, push the filling into the divisions so that they are full and rounded (Fig 2).

Turn in the open ends of the divisions

Summer tent

Once you have become accustomed to handling large areas of fabric, all kinds of simple projects become possible – such as a simple tent for the children to play in. The structure is basically three rectangles of fabric seamed together on the long sides. Two rectangles make the tent walls, the third makes the floor.

Support the tent ridge on the clothes line, making sure that the ends are properly secured.

Stitch ties to the bottom edges of the tent walls at intervals and tie them to pieces of wood pushed into the ground. Skewers with ring ends make even better tent pegs.

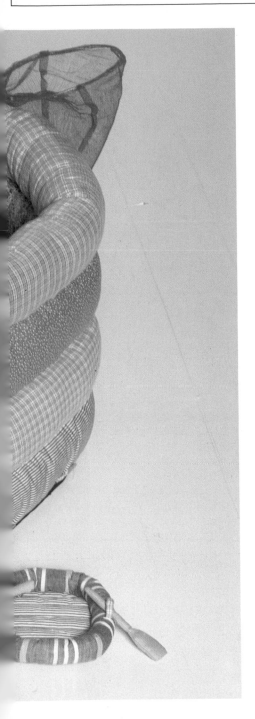

and close with Backstitching.

Cut the ribbon into eight pieces to make ties.

Sew the ties to the inside of the ring on each division, one on each side. The ties hold the ring together.

Following the technique described on page 4 (Fig 2) cut the square of fabric into a circle. Neaten the edges.

Sew the buttons equidistantly around the bottom edge of the lowest ring.

Make and stitch loops to the base circle to correspond with the buttons as shown in Fig 3.

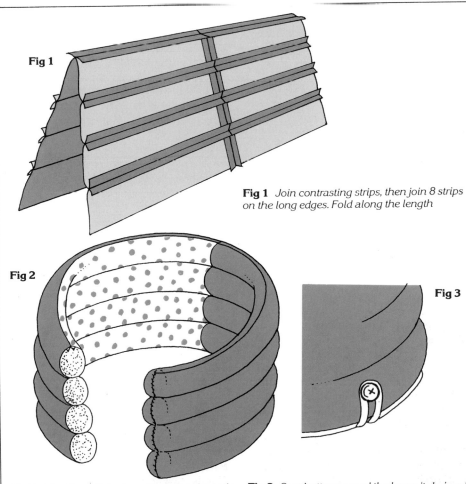

Fig 1 *Join contrasting strips, then join 8 strips on the long edges. Fold along the length*

Fig 2 *Machine-stitch along the seams through both thicknesses to make 'tubes'. Close one edge with slipstitches. Stuff the tubes*

Fig 3 *Sew buttons round the lower 'tube' and sew fabric or thread loops on the base circle to correspond to secure sides to base*

Wall pocket

The PVC material from which the wall pocket is made is not difficult to stitch. It can usually be obtained in bright colours as well as the clear type used for the pocket in the picture. Hang the wall pocket on the wall, behind the door or at the end of a bunk bed.

The wall pocket has thirteen pockets but more could be added. For instance, an extra pocket could be added on the top row, by re-spacing them, and the bottom row could be further subdivided.

Materials required

Finished size 75 × 60cm (30 × 24in)
120 × 75cm *(48 × 30in)* piece of PVC material
Packs of 12mm *(1/2in)*-wide bias binding, red, blue, green and yellow
Matching sewing threads
1m *(1 1/8yd)* of 12mm *(1/2in)*-diameter wooden dowelling
1m *(1 1/8yd)* thick cotton cord
Masking or adhesive tape

Preparation

From the PVC material, cut the main piece (A) 75 × 60cm *(30 × 24in)*. Cut a strip 60 × 30cm *(24 × 12in)*, (B). Cut a strip 60 × 10cm *(24 × 4in)*, (C). Cut three pockets 20 × 15cm *(8 × 6in)*, (D). (See Fig 1).

Making the wall pocket

Using machine-stitching, bind one long edge of strip B with bias binding (refer to page 38, Figs 1–3 for the technique for binding).

Bind both long edges of strip C. Bind

Shoe tidy

Make a useful shoe tidy using the same basic techniques as for the Wall Pocket. Cut the main piece 32.5 × 100cm *(13 × 40in)* and six pocket pieces 20cm *(8in)* square. Cut the pockets to shape as shown in the diagram. Mark the pocket positions as 20 × 12.5cm *(8 × 5in)* on the main piece, 6cm *(2 1/2in)* in from the sides, 6cm *(2 1/2in)* down from the top edge and 2.5cm *(1in)* apart. Bind the edges of the pockets and the main piece. Stitch the pockets to the marked positions, matching the side and bottom edges to the marked lines. Finish the tidy with tabs, a batten and a ribbon hanger.

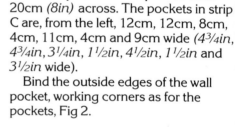

all four sides of the pockets D, using a different colour for each, (see picture). Do not attempt to mitre the corners. Simply bind along one side, cut off the binding level with the end and then bind the next side, leaving an overlap of about 6mm *(1/4in)* at the corner. When all four sides have been bound, turn the excess binding to the wrong side and catch with a few stitches (Fig 2).

Positioning the pockets

PVC material cannot be pinned or basted. Use self-adhesive tape to hold pieces together.

Lay the strips and pockets on the main piece A, following Fig 1. Tape in position. The D pockets lie 7cm *(2 3/4in)* from the top edge, with 4cm *(1 1/2in)* space between D and C and C and B.

Machine-stitch along the bottom edges of strips B and C and along the sides and bottom edges of pockets D.

Machine-stitch the pocket divisions.

The three pockets in strip B are each 20cm *(8in)* across. The pockets in strip C are, from the left, 12cm, 12cm, 8cm, 4cm, 11cm, 4cm and 9cm wide *(4 3/4in, 4 3/4in, 3 1/4in, 1 1/2in, 4 1/2in, 1 1/2in and 3 1/2in wide)*.

Bind the outside edges of the wall pocket, working corners as for the pockets, Fig 2.

Batten slots

From the remaining strip of PVC, cut 4 hanger pieces 23 × 4cm *(9 × 1 1/2in)*. Fold (without creasing) and tape the hangers to the top edge of the wall pocket, spacing them equidistantly, with the two outside edge hangers about 3cm *(1 1/4in)* from the edges. Machine-stitch the hangers, stitching over the binding stitching (Fig 3).

Slot the dowelling through the hangers. Knot the cord round the ends of the dowelling. Wind thread round the ends of the cord to prevent it ravelling.

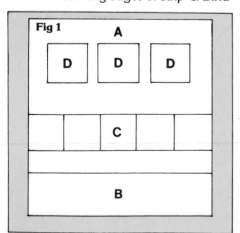

Fig 1 *Diagram of main piece A showing the pocket placements B, C and D*

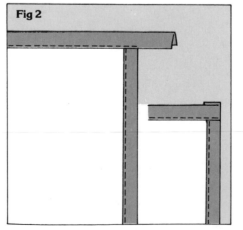

Fig 2 *Bind the sides of the wall-pocket, folding ends to the back at the corners*

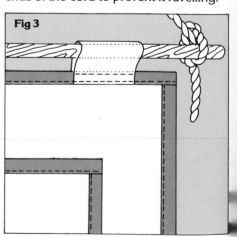

Fig 3 *Machine-stitch the hangers to the top edge, stitching over the binding stitching*

Outdoor Living

No matter how small it is, many people now try to turn their garden into an extra room in summer, eating around a table and relaxing in comfortable chairs. Outdoor living is now a way of life and in this chapter, you'll find ideas for making the most of garden furnishings.

Soft seating

Folding wooden garden chairs can be made more comfortable with a padded tie-on seat. Most wooden chairs of this type have 45cm *(18in)*-wide canvas seats but it is advisable to measure the chair before cutting the fabric.

Materials required

1.50m *(1⅝yd)* of 90cm *(36in)*-wide firmly-woven cotton fabric
50 × 20cm *(20 × 8in)* of the same or contrasting fabric for ties
Washable stuffing (polyester or polyurethane chips)
Matching sewing thread

Preparation

Cut the fabric in half lengthways. Cut four ties, 50 × 4cm *(20 × 1½in)*.

Making the seat

With right sides together, pin, baste and then machine-stitch the short ends and one long side.

Turn the seat to the right side and press. Topstitch the seams 6mm *(¼in)* from the edge.

Working from the top end, measure and pin 'pockets' for the stuffing, 23cm *(9in)* deep, with a 5cm *(2in)* strip between each pocket. Baste between the 'pockets', then work two rows of machine-stitching, ending the stitching 15mm *(⅝in)* from the open edge (see Fig 1). Fill the 'pockets' so that they are rounded, but do not overfill or the stitching may give way under the strain when the seat is being used.

Finishing

Turn the open edges of the side seam

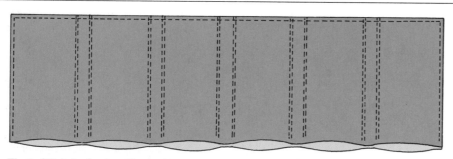

Fig 1 *Stitch the front and back pieces together on three sides, then turn and top-stitch on three sides. Stitch pocket divisions at approximately 22.5cm (9in) intervals, 5cm (2in) wide. Stuff the pockets*

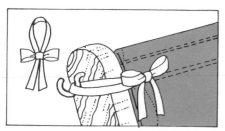

Fig 2 *Tie a looped bow in the fabric ties. Sew the bows to the division between the first and second sections. Loop the tie over a cuphook screwed into the chair side*

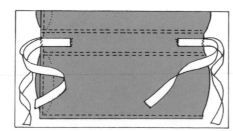

Fig 3 *Sew a folded tie to the underside of the seat, along the last division between sections. Tie the seat to the chair sides*

Sun bed

The soft seat pattern can also be used to make a portable sun bed or exercise mat.

Make the sun bed as instructed but instead of four ties, make two handles from 50 × 4cm *(20 × 1¹/₂in)* strips. Stitch the handles to the top edge of the sunbed and to the second machine-stitched strip down from the top end, on the underside.

Fold up the sun bed along the stitched strips and bring the handles together to carry it (see illustration).

to the inside, pin and baste. Top-stitch 6mm *(¹/₄in)* from the edge.

Fold and stitch four ties (refer to page 53, Fig 4 for the technique for making ties). Tie the ends of two into bows (see detail Fig 2) and then sew the bows to the seat on the edges of the first machine-stitched strip (Fig 2).

The loops are fastened over large hooks screwed into the chair frame.

The two remaining ties are folded and stitched to the underside of the seat, along the last stitched strip (see Fig 3). Tie the ends round the frame.

Two-faced cushions

Wooden or metal garden furniture looks attractive but can become a little uncomfortable to sit on after a time. Make a set of soft box cushions to fit the seat and, by using a different fabric on the front and back, a change of mood is easily achieved.

Box cushions also make casual floor seating when they are brought into the house in winter.

Estimating materials

The seat pictured has three square cushions, each 5cm (2in) thick. Measure the seat and cut foam block to size and shape as desired. If the seat is shaped, a paper pattern is made and used to cut the foam block to shape.

Fabrics Measure the foam block from front to back and from side to side. Add 3cm (1¼in) to each measurement.

For each two-sided cushion, you will need two pieces of fabric, each in a different pattern, to these dimensions, for the front and back of the cushion.

Measure the length and depth of one side of the block. Add 2.5cm (1in) to the measurements.

You will need two pieces to these dimensions from one fabric and two from the contrasting fabric, to make the cushion's box sides. Allow extra fabric for cutting bias strips for covering piping. This can be one of the two fabrics used, or can be a contrasting plain fabric.

Measure round the foam block, add 2.5cm (1in) and then double the measurement to estimate the amount of piping cord required for each cushion.

Materials required

5cm (2in)-thick foam block for each cushion

Two different fabrics for the cushion cover

Contrasting or matching fabric for covering piping

Piping cord

Matching sewing threads

Preparation

So that the cushion is reversible, two adjoining sides of the cushion are made

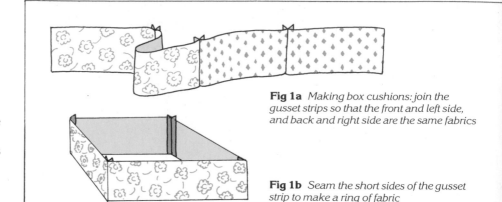

Fig 1a *Making box cushions: join the gusset strips so that the front and left side, and back and right side are the same fabrics*

Fig 1b *Seam the short sides of the gusset strip to make a ring of fabric*

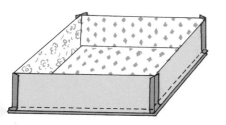

Fig 2 *Stitch the gusset to the cushion base, right sides facing, matching edges. Clip into the seam allowance at the corners for ease*

from the same fabric. Cut two sides from fabric A and two sides from fabric B.

Cut the top of the cushion from fabric A and the bottom side from fabric B.

Prepare and cover the piping following the technique described on page 10. Figs 2–6.

Making the box cushion

With right sides together, pin, baste and machine-stitch two side pieces of the same fabric together on the short ends. Press the seams open.

Join the two remaining side pieces in the same way. Machine-stitch the side pieces together to make the complete cushion sides (Fig 1).

Pin, baste and machine-stitch the prepared piping to the right side of the cushion front, raw edges matching. Join the ends of the piping as described on page 10 (Fig 6).

Pin and baste the prepared cushion sides to the cushion front, matching edges and corners, right sides facing.

Snip into the seam allowance at the corners of the side piece to ease the fabric (Fig 2). Machine-stitch all round, taking a 12mm (½in) seam. Remove the basting threads.

The bottom piece of the cushion cover is attached to the side piece in the same way. Pin, baste and machine-stitch the piping to the bottom cushion piece. Pin the sides and bottom piece together and baste. Machine-stitch starting about 5cm (2in) from a corner, round the corner and along two sides and then part of the fourth side. This leaves enough of the seam open to insert the foam block.

Turn the cushion cover to the right side. Put the foam block inside, easing it into the corners, and then hand-sew the open edges, using neat slipstitches.

Patchwork tablecloth

It is pleasant to have a special tablecloth for eating meals outdoors. The cloth pictured is designed for a square table and uses different fabrics, cut and stitched for a bright patchwork effect. Pieces of fabric left over from sewing projects can be used but it is advisable to use washable fabrics of similar weight and texture.

Materials required

Finished size 162cm (64in) square
80cm *(32in)* of 120cm *(48in)*-wide fabric A
75cm *(30in)* of 120cm *(48in)*-wide fabric B
Matching sewing threads
4 lead curtain weights

Preparation

From fabric A, cut one 38cm *(15in)* square (A), two 51cm *(20½in)* squares (D). Cut and join 10cm *(4in)*-wide strips to make four borders 164cm *(65in)* long (E), see Fig 1.

From fabric B, cut two 26cm *(10¼in)* squares (B), and two 37cm *(14½in)* squares (C), and two 73cm *(29in)* squares (E).

Cut all the squares, except square A, in half diagonally. All pieces include 12mm *(½in)* seam allowances.

Making the tablecloth

Machine-stitch triangles B to the sides of square A.

Stitch triangles C to the sides of new square B.

Stitch triangles D to the sides of new square C.

Stitch triangles E to the sides of new square D.

Stitch the borders E to the edges of the tablecloth. Cut the border ends diagonally and mitre the corners (see Fig 1).

Press all seams open as they are stitched.

Turn a narrow double hem on the cloth edges and machine-stitch.

Weighted corners

Corner weights will help to secure the cloth on windy days. Cut eight 7.5cm *(3½in)* circles from fabric B (cut out motifs if this is possible). Stitch two

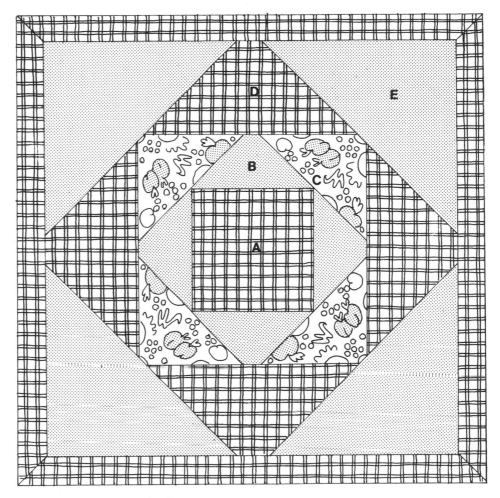

Fig 1 *Diagram for the construction of the patchwork cloth*

circles together right sides facing, turn to the right side and stuff with a cotton wool, pushing a weight into the middle. Close the seam with hand-sewing, inserting a 15cm *(6in)*-length of ribbon into the opening. Sew the other end of the ribbon to the cloth corner. Work four weights in the same way Fig 2.

Note: If closely woven fabrics are used there will be little fraying on the seam allowances. If fabrics are loosely woven, it will be necessary to neaten the seam allowances with zigzag-stitching.

Alternatively, the tablecloth can be lined with a plain fabric.

Squab cushions

Make a set of squab cushions for the garden chairs, to match the tablecloth.

Follow the instructions for making the Easy cushion on page 8 but add corner ties by basting a doubled strip of ribbon to the corners of the first cushion piece. Place the second cushion piece on top, right sides facing and stitch the seams.

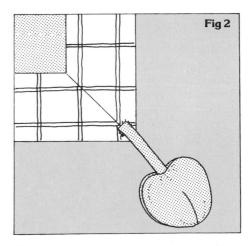

Fig 2 *Cut a motif from the fabric and cut the same shape from fabric. Sew together on the wrong side, turn and stuff, sewing a weight inside. Stitch to a ribbon and sew to the corners of the tablecloth*

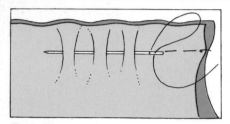
Fig 1 *Basting*

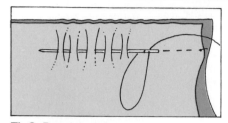
Fig 2 *Running stitch*

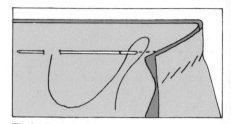
Fig 3 *Backstitch*

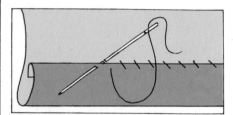
Fig 4 *Hemming*

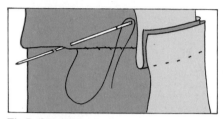
Fig 5 *Slipstitch*

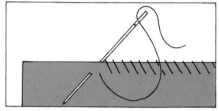
Fig 6 *Oversewing*

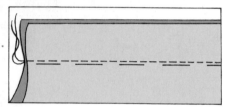
Fig 7 *Flat or straight seam*

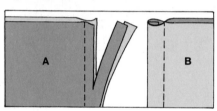
Fig 8 *French seam*

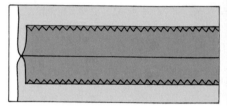
Fig 9 *Neatening a seam allowance*

Stitches and seams

Only a few stitches and seams are needed for the home sewing projects in this book.

Basting
This is used to hold two pieces of fabric together temporarily and also provides a guide to help you to achieve a straight seam.

Begin with a double Backstitch. Pick up 6mm (1/4in) stitches on the needle spacing them 6mm (1/4in) apart.

Running stitch
Running stitch has many uses in sewing. In this book it has been used for gathering.

Begin with a double Backstitch. Pick up several tiny stitches on the needle, all of the same length, with the same amount of fabric between stitches.

Backstitch
Backstitch can be used for working seams. Properly worked, it looks very like machine-stitching.

Begin with a double Backstitch, then bring the needle through from the back about 3mm (1/8in) forward along the seam line.

Re-insert the needle about 3mm (1/8in) behind the point where the thread came through and bring it out again 3mm (1/8in) forward on the seam line.

Continue inserting the needle at the end of the last stitch and bringing it through 3mm (1/8in) ahead.

Hemming
Hemming is used to hold hems in place. This is usually worked with the work held over the forefinger. Take a tiny stitch, then bring the needle diagonally through the edge of the hem. Space stitches 6mm (1/4in) apart.

Slipstitch
This is used to join two folded edges invisibly on hems and for attaching trims.

Bring the needle through just under the folded edge of fabric. Slide the needle through the fold for about 6mm (1/4in) then pick up a thread or two of the under fabric or adjacent fold.

Oversewing
This is used on raw edges to prevent them fraying.

Work from right to left or left to right. Work diagonally-placed stitches over the raw edge, keeping them evenly spaced and all of the same length.

Seams

Flat or straight seam
This is the most commonly used seam. Secure the machine thread with a few reverse stitches, then stitch beside the basting line. At the end of the seam, work a few reverse stitches.

French seam
This is used where raw edges are required to be enclosed for a neat finish or for a hard-wearing seam.

With wrong sides of fabric facing, stitch a seam 6mm (1/4in) from the edge. Trim the seam allowance (Fig 8a).

Re-fold the fabric so that right sides of fabric are together and stitch along the seam line (Fig 8b).

Neatening seam allowances
If the sewing machine has a zigzag stitch facility, work zigzag-stitching along the raw edges of the seam allowance after stitching the seam. Use oversewing if the neatening is to be done by hand.